The Amateur Astronomer
and his Telescope

GÜNTER D. ROTH M.A.G.

Director of the Lunar and Planetary Section
of the Vereinigung der Sternfreunde e.V., Germany

Translated by
ALEX HELM F.R.A.S.

D. VAN NOSTRAND COMPANY, INC.
Princeton, New Jersey
Toronto   London
New York

Made and printed in Great Britain by
William Clowes and Sons, Limited
London and Beccles

Contents

Illustrations

7

Illustrations

Illustrations

TEXT FIGURES

Foreword

There can be few people indeed who have never felt at least a passing interest in the science of astronomy. Some are quite content just to wonder and leave the matter at that; some will go so far as to read a little about the subject, but there are yet others who are anxious to investigate the mysteries of the heavens through a telescope with their own eyes. And it is with this latter group in mind that this book has been written.

Undoubtedly by far the best way of finding out about something is first hand experience. Astronomy is no exception, and a true appreciation of what goes on in the cosmos, and of the Earth's status in the universe, can really only be obtained at the telescope.

If one wishes to make full use of a telescope, one also has to have some knowledge of optics and a little engineering. In fact the amateur astronomer must be prepared to use his hands as well as his head. And, of course, the painstaking accuracy which practical observation demands is an excellent discipline for hand and mind.

No other branch of natural science can offer to the amateur such a wealth of opportunity for participating in practical work. Nor are amateur observers working in a vacuum, as it were, for the data recorded by amateurs all over the world have frequently formed the bases, or the proofs, of numerous theories.

The author has been connected with practical astronomy for amateur observers since 1947. He has gained a great deal of experience in organising amateur astronomers in Germany, and from his discussions with observers, both amateur and professional, and with teachers in all manner of schools he has learned a number of 'do's and don'ts'.

The writing of this book has been undertaken largely as a result of personal experiences in this respect. Therefore this book is not so much in the nature of a general handbook on astronomy, as a guide and, one hopes, inspiration to those who would like to tackle some simple astronomical tasks through practical work at the telescope.

Further reading is suggested in the footnotes and in the bibliography, and a list of relevant societies is also given.

The author would like to thank P. F. du Sautoy and Morley Kennerley, of Messrs. Faber & Faber, and Alex Helm for the English language edition of this book.

I

Choosing a Telescope

It need hardly be said that the first thing which will be needed is an astronomical instrument of some kind or another. Basically, there are two types of astronomical telescopes; those which collect the light from the stars by means of lenses are called *refractors*, while the other type, *reflectors*, use a curved mirror for gathering the rays of light. Each of these types has certain peculiar advantages and also disadvantages, and this particular point is not nearly so important as the size, when one is thinking about acquiring a telescope. For various reasons telescopes are not simply made to whatever dimensions might happen to come to mind, and in the course of time a number of fairly standard sizes of instruments suitable for the amateur have been evolved. Another important aspect which must enter into the considerations is the site where the instrument is to be used and type of mount on which it is to be placed, and then, of course, there is also the financial aspect. Telescopes of the kind used in large observatories entail such a vast capital outlay, both initially and in the upkeep, that they are completely out of the question for the private observer.

It is an odd fact that even in countries which have taken up the metric system the old-type units of measure still survive in astronomy to designate the diameters of telescopes. The optical efficiency of a telescope increases—though this is largely theoretical—with the size of the *effective aperture*, which is the actual surface area of the mirror or lens responsible for bringing the light rays to the eye-lens. A small proportion of the nominal aperture is usually obscured by the fittings which hold the lens or mirror in place in the telescope tube. The two units of measure most commonly met with to indicate the diameter of lens or mirror are the Paris inch ($=27.1$ mm) and the British standard inch ($=25.4$ mm). The Paris unit is used mainly for smaller instruments up to about eight inches diameter, but any confusion can always be resolved by quoting the effective aperture of a particular instrument in millimetres.

Assuming that two telescopes possess equally good optics, there will be no noticeable difference in the performance of one, say, 75 mm diameter and one of 80 mm. Only when the difference in the diameters becomes at all considerable, something in the nature of 50 mm or so (approximately 2 inches), will this difference between the two instruments become at all apparent. Thus to the initiated the diameter of a telescope quoted in inches places the instrument into a particular category, and the terms two-, four-, or six-inch give a good indication of the performance of which the particular instrument is capable.

At this stage, let us consider what is meant by magnification, or *power*. For practical purposes this may be calculated from the formula:

$$P = \frac{f_o}{f_E}$$

where P is the power, f_o the focal length of the object-lens or main mirror, and f_E the focal length of the eyepiece.

One sometimes comes across the term 'normal power',

a value calculated from the ratio between the diameter of the objective and the diameter of the pupil of the eye; for the purpose of such calculations the diameter of the pupil in night conditions is taken as 6 mm (0.24 inches). With normal power all the available light is assumed to reach the eye; thus any increase above this value necessarily entails some loss in brightness when the subject under observation is one which shows a disc. In contrast, for stellar observations normal magnifications up to ×6 can in fact increase the range. A magnification which is greater than one-and-a-half times the aperture of the instrument measured in millimetres (e.g. for a six-inch = 150 mm a magnification greater than ×225) is virtually useless since it actually exceeds the resolving power of the objective. It is as well to know something about these things since they help to establish the limits of a particular instrument, and this in turn may influence the choice.

Anyone who is about to equip himself with a telescope should ask himself three questions:

1. For what sort of observations is the instrument to be used?
2. Where is the instrument to be sited?
3. How much can I afford?

Those who merely wish to glance at the heavens from time to time, and show their friends and relations the Moon, will probably find a two- or three-inch refractor ample for their needs. Instruments of this kind are nowadays to be had complete with carrying cases, which enables them to be transported easily and erected whenever they are required. Another advantage is that such instruments are fairly robust, and tiny fingers activated by enquiring minds cannot wreak much damage; by contrast, a reflector is in many ways a far more delicate piece of apparatus, and can easily be thrown out of alignment. If, on the other hand, it is the intention to mount the instrument in one's garden, and to pursue systematic observations of the Moon and/or the planets, perhaps even to photograph these bodies, the owner will be best advised to go in for a long-focus instrument having a diameter of at least six inches, either a Cassegrain or a Newtonian reflector. A permanent mount can then be set up, and a shelter of some kind constructed to protect the instrument from the ravages of the weather.

Those amateur astronomers who are looking for something out of the ordinary run of instruments may prefer telescope designs such as 'Schupmann Medial', 'Cassegrain-Maksutov', or 'Schmidt Reflector', three very interesting types of instruments with exceedingly fine optics. Any qualified optical engineer engaged in the construction or sale of telescopes will probably be competent to advise on these designs

The type of mount which will have to be used for the instrument is another important factor in the choice of telescope. Unfortunately this is a point which is often ignored until the last moment, with the result that, in the quest for bigger and better optics, many an enthusiast has been bitterly disappointed when it comes to siting and mounting the instrument. Whatever people may tell you, it is utter fallacy that any telescope with a diameter greater than four inches may be kept transportable; there are bound to be serious snags, and not even a light aluminium stand and a fairly firm reflecting system can make the situation any better. I write from bitter experience over nine long years of struggle with these

. 110 mm. Brachyt Reflector belonging to the author, $f = 1 : 20$, with
quatorial mount on concrete pillar. The instrument is situated in the
attic of an ordinary detached house.

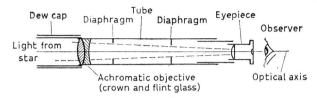

a. Achromatic refractor.

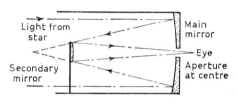

b. Newtonian reflector.

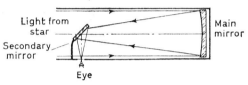

c. Cassegrain reflector.

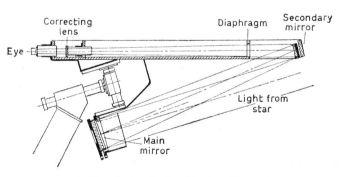

d. Brachyt reflector (Anton Kutter).

Fig. 1. The principal types of telescopes.

so-called portable stands for first of all a three-inch Merz refractor, and then a four-inch Brachyt reflector. Using these instruments in this fashion led to a great deal of frustration one way or another, and I strongly recommend setting up a permanent mount either in the garden or on the roof, if this is in any way possible. There is no need to go to the expense of a proper observatory with revolving dome and so forth.

If a permanent mount is out of the question, then a portable mount is, of course, the only alternative, but, if this is the case, it will be as well to restrict oneself to an instrument whose diameter does not exceed four inches. In fact it might be as well to consider whether a really good pair of binoculars would not be more worth while. Not that this is intended to be at all patronising towards the users of binoculars. In some fields of astronomy they are able to render very valuable service indeed. In addition, binoculars also have the advantage that they need not be used solely for astronomical purposes, while in the normal course of events astronomical reflectors and refractors cannot be used for admiring the view.

Anyone buying a pair of binoculars with the intention of using them occasionally for astronomical observation should make sure that the instrument he acquires not only has sufficiently good light-gathering power, but also suitable magnification. The figures 6 × 30 engraved on a pair of binoculars indicate that the instrument has an aperture of 30 mm and a magnification of × 6; 10 × 50 an aperture of 50 mm and a magnification of × 10. The product of the object-lens aperture and the magnification gives us a measure of performance assuming dusk conditions; this is the significant factor for astronomical work. With very powerful binoculars, 12 × 60, one can make out stars down to magnitude 11 or 12 on clear moonless nights, providing that there is no interference from street lighting and the like; in similar conditions an instrument 6 × 30 will show stars down to magnitude 10. Rather than just using the instrument held in the hand, it is advisable to clamp the binoculars to a ball and socket fixed to a tripod, similar to the arrangement used for ciné-cameras. The observer using binoculars needs to know the area of the field of vision; with instruments marked 6 × 30 or 8 × 30 this is usually about 8–9 degrees, or, to put it more graphically, roughly equivalent to the apparent distance between the stars *Beta* and *Kappa* in the constellation Orion. Against this, an instrument marked 12 × 60 will enable one to get just the three stars forming the belt of Orion in the same field. While a pair of binoculars can be used successfully for certain aspects of stellar astronomy, such as star-counting, or the observation of star-fields and star-clusters, it must be realised that one cannot use high magnifications, and one would therefore have to for-go any work which entails study of details on, say, the Moon or the planets.

For such purposes one inevitably requires a telescope of larger dimensions, and this in turn may be successfully applied to a number of different fields. A three- or four-inch refractor is generally regarded as a good starting instrument for the serious amateur observer, while for a reflector the aperture can be increased to as much as six to eight inches without incurring any extra cost or technical difficulties. This does not mean that the performance of a four-inch refractor is equivalent to that of an eight-inch reflector. The difference in quality between a refractor and a reflector of equal diameter (from about four inches upwards) is, in any case, based more on theoretical than on practical considerations. Generally it is the secondary mirror in a reflector which causes the greatest headaches, such as loss of light and silhouetting. Thus from the outset larger diameters are called for, and the smaller reflecting telescopes of something like two or three inches diameter are hardly worth the money spent on them.

Reflecting telescopes are more susceptible to atmospheric turbulences than are refractors, and it is by no means an easy task to align and adjust the optical system. So far as the durability of the main reflecting surface is concerned, I can say from personal experience that a good aluminium coating can last from eight to ten years without deteriorating, even in urban areas. The alleged 'weaknesses' of reflecting systems are—and again I speak from personal experience—not really worth bothering about. In fact they tend to sink very much into the background when one compares the cost of a reflecting system with that of a good object-lens. Some reflectors, such as the Cassegrain and the Brachyt, also have the additional advantage in that they possess a long focal length combined with a short structural length. However where the reflector really does score over the refractor is in the matter of colour aberration. Such an effect occurs only in refractors, where white light on passing through the object lens is split into its component colours. This happens because those light rays having a short wave length (blue) are bent more abruptly by the lens than those with a long wave length (red), and, while this fault can be reduced to some extent, it can never be eliminated entirely. In consequence a refractor has a visual, as well as a photographic, focus, since it is usually corrected for visual work. A reflector, on the other hand, is equally efficient both for photographic and for direct observation, because all the light rays in the long and short wave range are brought to the same focal point.

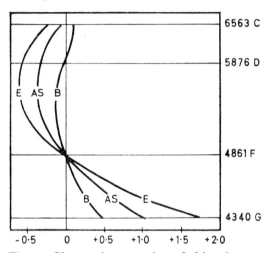

Fig. 2. Chromatic correction of object-lenses. The vertical axis shows the wave lengths, and the horizontal the differences in focal lengths in mm with an object-lens focus of 1000 mm (secondary spectrum).

E = normal Zeiss achromatic object-lens.
AS = semi-apochromatic lens by Zeiss.
B = Apochromatic lens by Zeiss.

The critical factor for every refractor is the suppression of the *secondary spectrum*. Simple achromatic lenses (flint-glass lens plus crown-glass lens) unfortunately do not satisfy every requirement. The important point here is that achromatism can really be achieved for no more than two colours at a time. In other words, only two well-defined wave lengths of the visible spectrum can be brought to the same focus. The other colours, which remain unaffected, then show up as the secondary spectrum; the foci for these therefore will lie either in front of, or behind, the focus chosen for achromatic correction. Compared with the usual Fraunhofer achromatic lenses, semi-apochromatic object-lenses constitute a marked improvement. While in the former the secondary spectrum accounts for about 0·3% of the total focal length, in a good semi-apochromatic lens this value has been halved to 0·15%. An exceptionally high level of correction has been attained in triple-lens apochromates (only about 0·05%). But, needless to say, such improvements can only be achieved with higher cost.

For the sort of apertures which the ordinary amateur is able to handle with ease (say, about six inches, i.e. 150 mm), he should find himself amply served by a simple achromatic, and most certainly by a semi-apochromatic object lens. At such an aperture and the corresponding focal length the secondary spectrum is kept within reasonable limits. Most instruments of this sort are constructed so that the aperture ratio is about 1:15; indicating that the focal distance is 15 times the diameter of the object-lens.

Basically, the demands on the quality of the optical components of a telescope, whether this be refractor or reflector, increase with the aperture ratio. While reflecting telescopes with aperture ratios ranging between 1:10 and 1:20 can easily make do with simpler and cheaper spherical mirrors, reflecting systems of 1:8, or even 1:6 require parabolic reflecting surfaces for the main mirror; these are more difficult and hence also more expensive to produce. Although instruments of this kind having short focal lengths may at first sight seem attractive, because of their compactness, it is on the whole advisable to look for aperture ratios somewhere in the region of 1:10 or 1:20. While on this point, it is well to remember that the normal conceptions of light values, such as we come across in photography, do not really apply here. So far as astronomical telescopes are concerned, if these are employed principally for visual work, such values apply only in a very limited sense. The thing to note is that the effective aperture is the critical factor for the resolution and definition of the telescope, and this is particularly important.

Furthermore, given the choice, the instrument having the longer focal length should always be given preference, even though the aperture ratio might sink as low as 1 : 20. So far as the magnification is concerned, the longer focal length of the main mirror or lens permits the use of eyepieces which also have a long focal length. This tends to make the actual business of observing more comfortable. In addition, an aperture ratio of 1 : 15 or 1 : 20 does not in the least preclude the photographing of bright objects, such as the Moon, the Sun, or some of the planets. And in any case, when it comes to photographing star-clusters and distant nebulæ not even a ratio of 1 : 6 is much help; for such purposes special equipment is necessary.

In the post-war period, do-it-yourself telescope construction has found increasing popularity. 'Amateur Telescope Making'* has caught on not only in the New World, but also in the Old. As well as providing an interesting and absorbing hobby, this has the added advantage that the resulting instrument costs very much less than a ready-made one. Some people are sufficiently

---

* A. G. Ingalls has published a work in three volumes under this title (Scientific American, New York, 1953) which deals with practically any problem the amateur telescope maker might encounter.

gifted with their hands to be able to build a telescope right from scratch, doing everything themselves, including the grinding of the optics; others may not want, or be able, to go to quite such lengths, and will content themselves with making just the tube and the mount, having bought the optics already made. In this way many an amateur has been able to acquire an eight-, ten- or even twelve-inch instrument—chiefly of the reflecting variety. However, even an experienced do-it-yourselfer should remember that the sheer size of his telescope will not necessarily make a second Kepler of him, and what began as an early enthusiasm may well turn into an addiction. While I have a very high regard for those who are never quite one hundred per cent content with what they have achieved and are constantly improving their handiwork, I do feel that the construction of a telescope should only ever be regarded as a means to an end, at least for the serious observer.

On the purely economic side, it seems that it is possible to build for oneself a reflecting telescope with a diameter of six or eight inches for something like £50 or so. It is also possible to achieve extremely high quality, as has been amply demonstrated by one particular group of amateurs in Schaffhausen in Switzerland, to mention but one instance. Even if one buys a mirror system ready made (the complete optics for a six-inch Newtonian or Cassegrain reflector can be obtained nowadays for around £40–50) and then has the remaining parts built to specification by a competent engineer, one can still obtain a medium-sized instrument which will be relatively cheap at the price—especially when one considers that a brand-new refractor of three inches diameter, complete with mount and so forth, can easily cost more than £100.

II

The Equatorial Mount

The same care ought always to be applied to the choice of mount as the actual telescope. Unfortunately this is often not the case. Anyone who has tried to observe for any length of time through a telescope without an adequate stand will bear out the fact that this is, to say the least of it, downright uncomfortable. Even an ordinary tripod can help. If, however, a four-inch refractor or a six-inch reflector is to be used, then a simple tripod is not quite the right solution. If nothing else, it is good practice for a beginner to try out his instrument on an ordinary altazimuth mount. Sun, Moon and planets, as well as all other celestial bodies, will be seen to participate in some wild and weird dance in the field of vision, that is to say even if the desired object can be easily located in the first place.

As a general rule, the bearing axes of the mount should never be too delicate; it is far better to have them slightly more robust than is strictly necessary. Later on we shall probably want to add all sorts of other items to our telescope, and a solid mounting is then even more essential. Furthermore, the centre of gravity of the telescope on its stand should always lie as close as possible to the point where the two axes, declination and right ascension, intersect. Where this is not the case, the disadvantages are not always immediately apparent, but it will be found that during long time-exposures in photographic work the guidance is not entirely accurate.

Fundamentally there are two sorts of mounts for telescopes. There is first of all the simple altazimuth mount of the kind found used with terrestrial telescopes, where the instrument can be moved in two planes, vertical and horizontal. This is fine for gazing at one's surroundings, and is also suitable for astronomical work requiring no more than small magnification (i.e. binoculars). But anyone wishing to work with higher magnifications will soon discover that it is no easy matter to keep the subject of the observation in the centre of the field of vision. The apparent diurnal motion of all the bodies in the heavens is due to the rotation of the Earth upon its axis. Thus with an altazimuth mount, adjustment has constantly to be made about two axes, and it is surprising how rapidly the Earth does spin. This phenomenon is particularly noticeable if one is observing one of the planets, say Mars or Jupiter, using a power of about × 200; no sooner has one got one's victim centred, than it is almost out of view again.

With a small magnification and a wide angle of vision the ability to keep the subject of observation more or less in the middle of the field does not matter quite so much, but with increasing magnification and the corresponding restriction of the field of vision, easy and exact following becomes more and more desirable, while for most photographic projects it is an absolute necessity.

The other type, known as the parallactic or equatorial mount, is the ideal for astronomical telescopes. It works in the following manner: we again have two axes, polar and declination; the polar axis lies parallel to the Earth's axis, and thus points in the direction of the celestial

26

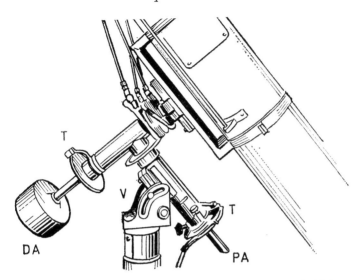

Fig. 3. A typical equatorial mount. PA = polar axis, DA = declination axis, T = setting circles; the angle of the polar axis can be adjusted at V.

pole—marked approximately by the Pole Star—making an angle with the plane of the horizon which corresponds to the geographic latitude of the point of observation; conversely, of course, the latitude of the site of the telescope determines the angle of the polar axis. The declination axis lies at right angles to the polar axis, about which it is able to rotate. If we now set the declination axis so that the telescope is pointing towards a given star, then the instrument can be made to follow this star in its apparent movement across the sky simply by rotating it about the polar axis. The instrument in fact describes what is known as the declination or parallel arc. Declination indicates the distance of a body from the celestial equator, and is measured in degrees of arc. Once the declination has been set, it is necessary only to swing the

instrument in right ascension—i.e. about the polar axis—
to compensate for the Earth's rotation, and so retain
the object under observation in the centre of the field of
vision.

Thus with an equatorial mount, movement about only
the one axis is sufficient to ensure a reliable following of a
given object, and fully compensates for the apparent
diurnal motion of the celestial sphere. Equatorial mounts
have yet another advantage; calibrated circles can be
fitted to indicate the declination and right ascension of
the instrument. In this way, if one looks up the position of
a given body in an appropriate table, and sets the
instrument accordingly, the desired object should then be
in the centre of the field of vision. This is especially useful
if one wishes to observe during the hours of daylight, and
also obviates the need to scan the sky to find very
faint objects. The right ascension scale is to be found on
the polar axis, and is calibrated in hours (equivalent to
divisions of 15 degrees of arc). The declination circle is
fixed to the other axis, and is usually marked off in degrees of arc reading from zero through 360 degrees.
Sometimes there are two zero points, 180 degrees apart,
and the scale then reads 90 degrees in either direction
from each of these. Each circle has a fixed indicator, and
for even greater accuracy occasionally a vernier scale.

Setting circles are wonderful gadgets, which are absolutely indispensable for really large telescopes. However, I doubt whether, in fact, they are at all necessary
for the usual run of instruments owned by amateur observers. Here they are really not all that important in
practice, and, in any case, unless the circles are sufficiently large there is bound to be some loss of precision in
reading off the calibrations. At any rate, the presence of

such circles should not influence one unduly in the choice of telescope or mount. The actual form of the mount can vary considerably, although the principle naturally remains the same. Apart from the usual 'German' design, there is also the 'English' type, as well as 'Springfield' mount, which enables the observer to view always from the same position.

To my mind, the greatest sin is to possess an equatorial mount and then not to set it up correctly. It need hardly be said that in this condition the telescope is even more difficult to handle than it would be if it were on a simple altazimuth stand. Even an amateur observer, who is forced through circumstances to reassemble his telescope and mount every time he wants to observe, need not necessarily deprive himself of the joys of an equatorial mount; naturally, life becomes a great deal easier if one is able to rig up some sort of permanent 'observatory'. Such structures may vary from a sort of garden-shed affair, where the roof is either rolled back, or folds down—Patrick Moore at East Grinstead, for instance has a shed mounted on rollers, so that the whole thing can be rolled back to leave the telescope standing clear—to something more elaborate built into the roof of one's house. Necessity is invariably the mother of invention in this respect, and one method is as good as another, provided it does the job. If advice be needed, it is that one must not forget to leave oneself enough room to work comfortably.

How then does one go about setting up an equatorial mount?

Let us first of all assume that we have decided on a permanent site for the instrument in the garden, where the view to the south, east and west is reasonably unobstructed. The actual stand on which the mounting is to be fixed can consist either of a concrete plinth, or a heavy tripod (sometimes of wood, sometimes of iron), or simply a wooden pillar, this latter being the type often supplied by makers of astronomical instruments as a standard component. It cannot be stressed too often that whatever type of stand is used, it should be as rigid as possible. Ideally, of course, natural rock-bed is best, but an excellent alternative is a concrete foundation, sunk six feet into the ground if necessary, though much depends on the size of the instrument and the type of soil. Pillars made of bricks, building blocks, or wooden beams have a number of drawbacks, and experience has shown that a cast-iron tube filled with concrete and firmly embedded in a compressed concrete footing of adequate depth gives by far the best service; the actual equatorial is then fitted atop this pillar. Where a tripod is supplied it is better to stand this on a concrete raft rather than the soft earth.

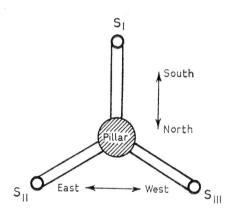

Fig. 4. Position of the feet of an equatorial mount; the levelling screws are at S_I S_{II} S_{III}.

The Equatorial Mount

At the foot of the stand, or the mount itself, three adjustment screws will be found. These enable the mount to be levelled, and also help us to obtain a fine setting for the polar axis. Two of these screws should be placed on a line running east–west, so that the third then points due south. Next, fix the mount and the telescope to the stand in such a way that the polar axis lies along a line running north–south, and points more or less in the direction of the Pole Star. This can be done during the day when one can see what one is doing. Having obtained a rough setting, the next thing to do is to focus the telescope on the Sun. Here, however, I must add a word of warning. NEVER look directly at the Sun through binoculars or a telescope, for this can lead to serious injury to the eyes, even ultimately resulting in blindness. A solar diagonal or pentaprism is one answer to the problem (see p. 69), but a far simpler method is to project the image of the Sun on to a screen held a little way away from the eyepiece. It is not very difficult to manufacture some sort of contrivance to clamp on to the telescope in order to keep the screen, consisting of a piece of white card, in place. Once the Sun is centred in the field of vision, lock the declination axis. The instrument is now free to turn only on the polar axis in order to follow the apparent motion of the Sun. A few minutes should show us whether the mount has been set correctly. If it has, then the image of the Sun will continue to occupy the centre of the field; if not it will tend to move either out of the top of the field, or the bottom. A slight adjustment to the angle of the polar axis, or its direction—trial and error here is a better teacher than any book—and we should be able to prevent too rapid a drift of the Sun's image from the field of vision.

The Equatorial Mount

However, this is still only a rough setting, and we must next apply what is known as the Scheiner test, so called after an astronomer of that name. This not only ensures that the mount has been set up accurately, but also that all the mechanical parts function properly. A very slight divergence does not really matter all that much for small amateur telescopes, and can often be compensated for by a twist of one of the adjustment screws.

This operation takes place at night. A brightish star near the meridian, that is to say in the south (to those observing from the Earth's northern hemisphere), is brought into the field of vision. Very carefully we adjust the declination and the right ascension until the star is exactly in the centre of the field in the telescope. The job is made all the easier if one has an eyepiece with a hair-line cross. To start with one should use a moderate magnification, or *power* as it is often called; say about × 20 for every inch of aperture. Having now centred the star, the declination is clamped tight; the instrument is thus free to follow the star in right ascension only. So that the telescope may be swung slowly and evenly, a slow-motion drive is fitted to the polar axis; sometimes the declination axis also has a slow-motion drive, but if the instrument has been set up correctly there should be no real need for this.

The experiment is virtually the same as the one carried out in daylight with the Sun. The effect is also likely to be the same; after a short while it will probably be found that the star will begin to wander away, upward or downward, from the central line. If the star tries to escape upwards, i.e. increasing declination, then this is a sign that the polar axis points a little to the west of the meridian (north–south line). The matter can soon be put right

O. R. Knab

III. 6″ Newtonian reflector, $f = 1 : 4$. The instrument has a high light-gathering power for use with low magnifications. The tube is made from aluminium, and the instrument belongs to Oscar R. Knab, South Bend, U.S.A.

F. Grau

IV. Stand for binoculars 22×80, with couch for observing.

V. Revolving dome with slit, made from sheet metal.

VI. H. Vehrenberg's private observatory in the Black Forest. The roof of the shed simply folds back to either side.

by turning the mount *gently* in an anti-clockwise direction. The important point to note is that the adjustment screw in the foot lying on the meridian (i.e. facing south) must on no account be moved.

If the star appears to move downward from the line, i.e. decreasing declination, then the polar axis is pointing to the east of the meridian line, and this can be put right by turning the mount carefully in a clockwise direction. At this juncture it should be mentioned that, because the image in an astronomical telescope is inverted, north appears at the bottom of the field, south at the top, while west and east are left and right respectively when one is looking southward of the zenith.

The mount will, in all probability, have to be turned this way and that several times before the optimum position is found. If the star remains centrally placed in the field of vision for not less than half an hour, then the first part of the operation may be regarded as successfully concluded. This brings us to the next point: testing the polar altitude, in other words finding out if the extension of the polar axis passes through the celestial pole.

To do this we have to find a fairly prominent star situated approximately six hours east of the meridian, and having positive declination—here it is best to consult a star chart. It will have to be a star which has only just risen. Again we go through the familiar motions: centre the star in the field; clamp the declination, and follow in right ascension, observing the while how the star behaves. Any deviation upwards or downwards signifies an error in the polar altitude, i.e. the angle of the polar axis. If the star appears to rise, the angle is too acute. The answer is to lower the adjustment screw set in the foot on the meridian. Conversely, if the star sinks in the field correction is made by turning the same adjustment screw the other way (clockwise). The process of adjusting this set screw should be carried out with the utmost care; give the screw no more than about a quarter of a turn at a time.

To be really safe, the same test may be carried out on a star six hours to the west of the central meridian. Here it must be remembered that the opposite effects occur; if the star appears to rise in the field of vision, then the angle is too great, and so on.

With a little patience and practice it is not difficult for anyone to become reasonably expert at setting up an equatorial mount. Should the instrument have to be dismantled, so as to keep it transportable, the best thing is to mark the places where the adjustment screws have to go, and even to mark the screws themselves in order to facilitate subsequent re-erection. Another, and possibly better, idea is to fix a circular level (bubble) to the mount, and to set this rigidly once the angle and direction of the polar axis have been fixed. The position of the bubble can then be used as a guide when the instrument is again assembled. One simply places the feet of the screws into three little dents in the surface on which the mount is usually erected—for instance one could cement in three metal discs, even tin lids, though brass would be better since it does not rust—and all that is then required is to adjust the screws so that the bubble again comes to a marked spot.

If one is careful enough in carrying out this Scheiner test, the instrument will be found to fulfil all the demands made of it; this applies even to photographic work, where the subject has to be followed over long periods of exposure. The results will be found perfectly satisfactory and reliable.

The Equatorial Mount

Sometimes it is possible to convert an altazimuth mount so that it acts as an equatorial. All that has to be done is to tilt the base plate so that it lies at an angle, which we shall call *a* (alpha), to the horizontal. This angle *a* is equivalent to 90 degrees *minus* the geographical latitude of the site from which the observation is being made. Naturally this method must not be regarded as a permanent solution, and in any case is really only applicable to small instruments. Where larger telescopes are concerned the stability of the whole set-up is endangered, and it would be a shame to have to salvage the remains of a sizable telescope from the ground merely for the sake of an equatorial mount—and one which did not succeed at that.

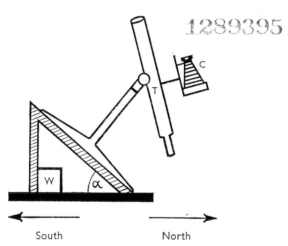

South   North

Fig. 5. A simple conversion to enable altazimuth stands to be used equatorially: Angle *alpha* = 90 degrees **minus** the latitude of the observatory; the telescope (T) and camera (C) on the altazimuth stand are inclined at the angle *alpha* as shown. The stand can be mounted on a board and held secure by means of a weight (W).

III

Optional Extras

It is often said that it is not the telescope itself which is expensive, but the bits and pieces which one adds to it in the course of time. This is, of course, true, but it is the same in any serious hobby—such as photography, where a simple camera is after a time found wanting, and one feels compelled to acquire interchangeable lenses, filters for this and that, exposure meters and so on and so forth; it is the same with cars, where fog-lamps, windscreen washers and the like are accessories we indulge in; some—we claim—are indispensable, others sheer luxury. The trimmings are not always very expensive in any case, and both inspiration and value can be found in the advertising columns of the various scientific periodicals. Very often just those optical components for which the amateur is looking are to be found among ex-government stock; in fact entire telescopes have been built from bits and pieces acquired in this way.

There are several items no amateur observer should be without right from the start: the finder and a selection of eyepieces. Admittedly there are some keen enthusiasts who consider that a finder is an unnecessary extravagance. They prefer, optically speaking of course, to 'fire over open sights'. While such a method might be quite adequate for something like a two-inch instrument, so far as anything larger is concerned it ceases to be practical, and, if the telescope is a reflector of the Newtonian or Brachyt type, such an arrangement is definitely no joke, for on these one does not look into the eyepiece in the direction in which the instrument is pointing. Only in the course of time will one come to appreciate the practical value of a good finder with a fairly wide field of vision and a sighting grid.

The finder does not need to have anything as elaborate as an apochromatic object lens; in fact the simplest lens will do for the purpose. An old photographic lens with a focus of about 20–30 cm and an aperture ratio of about 1 : 8 is neither difficult to obtain nor very expensive nowadays. Good value for money are what are called monoculars, which, as their name implies, are half-binoculars. They often have hair-line sights which make them ideal finders for telescopes ranging between two and six inches diameter. Any optician will be able to supply such an instrument, or possibly one of the government surplus stores.

The finder should be attached to the main instrument in such a way that an object in the centre of its field of vision also lies at the centre of the field in the telescope, but the finder field will, of course, be much larger, depending on the magnification being used.

À propos of this matter of magnification, it is virtually useless to try to use a telescope properly with only one magnification or power, and every observer should have at least three eyepieces to hand. The degree of magnification is given by dividing the focal length of the eyepiece into the focal length of the optical system of the telescope. The focal length of the eyepiece will usually be found engraved on it or its cap, and is measured in millimetres. Thus the three eyepieces should be chosen in such a way as to give a convenient range of magnifications: (1) between ×30 and ×60; (2) between ×80 and ×120; (3) between ×150 and ×200. If one is fortunate enough to be able to afford additional eyepieces, the best thing is to extend this range at either end; at the top end an eyepiece to give a magnification of about ×300 and at the lower end something like ×20.

It is wrong to imagine that a high power is necessarily much better than a low one. Each type of eyepiece has its own specific use, as well as a definite influence on the quality of the image obtained. A poor eyepiece, or the wrong sort, can ruin the performance of even the best reflector or refractor. There are many eyepieces which have

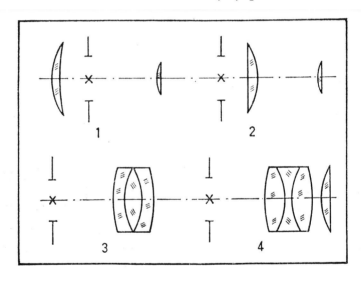

Fig. 6. Section through eyepieces: (1) Huygens type, (2) Ramsden type, both of which provide fairly good optical quality and a satisfactory field of vision at relatively low cost, (3) monocentric type, and (4) orthoscopic type, both of which place a high demand on spherical and chromatic correction.

been specially corrected to meet certain specific demands. As a general rule instruments having a large ratio (1:6 to 1:10) require lenses with a greater degree of correction, while long-focus systems with small aperture ratios (1:11 to 1:20) can manage with simpler types. It should be added, however, that for observing objects which show discs, such as the Moon and the planets, with a high power, ane yepiece with full chromatic correction should always be given preference. Such eyepieces are called 'orthoscopic' or 'monocentric'. Simple examples of eye-pieces are the Huyghenian and the Mittenzwey lenses, the latter variety having a particularly wide apparent field of vision (50 degrees).*

A hair-cross sight is always a useful accessory for an observer, and this is another factor which must be considered when choosing eyepieces. Among other things, the hair cross constitutes a simple form of micrometer; this is a device which enables us to measure in the telescopic field small differences in position of two points in the heavens. Apart from using an eyepiece with a built-in hair cross, it is also possible to fix one separately in the focal plane of the telescope, so that it can be used with any number of different eyepieces. The only snag is that the eyepiece then has to be one that has its focus shortly in front of the convex lens (Ramsden or micrometer type lens). In eyepieces where the focus lies between the convex and the actual eye lens, it is best to fix the hair cross to the diaphragm within the eyepiece itself.

To do this the ring diaphragm must be removed and marked with four equidistant notches, i.e. at 90 degree

* Details of these and other types of eyepieces are given by H. E. Dall on p. 78 of the *Yearbook of Astronomy*, 1963, published by Eyre & Spottiswoode at 15*s*.

intervals. The notches lying opposite to each other are then connected with a hair, or some other fine filament, so as to form a cross at the centre of the ring, with the two filaments at right angles to each other. The fixing of the hair lines to the ring can be accomplished in the same way that the latter is itself fixed to the eyepiece, namely with a little artificial resin glue. The diaphragm then has to be fixed back in the eyepiece in such a way that the hair cross appears absolutely sharp when one looks through the eyepiece. I have also managed to draw out fine filaments from the resin glue itself, to use as the hair lines; the advantage of these is that, being slightly translucent, they show up better in the dark. This fact makes them particularly suitable for use in the finder. Too often the hair cross cannot be distinguished against the dark background of the sky, and it is helpful to illuminate the cross slightly. For this purpose a well-masked torch bulb (only a minimum of light is desirable) can be fixed to one side of the finder eyepiece, or the eyepiece draw tube of the main instrument, in such a way that its shaded light is thrown directly in front of the eyepiece.

In other methods the field of vision is illuminated by means of a small glass tube containing luminous material, or by making the filaments of the cross from luminous or fluorescent matter. It is possible even to apply a little luminous paint to an existing hair line.

An accessory which can save a great deal of neck-ache is a zenith prism. However, if your instrument is to be a Newtonian reflector, this will not concern you; instead a sturdy pair of steps is likely to be the answer, though this will depend on the size of the instrument and the type of stand on which it is mounted. A zenith prism is intended mainly for use with the type of telescope where one looks in at the bottom end, and its purpose is to make the observation of objects situated between about 45 degrees declination and the zenith far more comfortable. Those who can put up with being martyrs to their hobby will find that they are able to do without this piece of equipment.

An earth-clock, that is to say a mechanical drive to compensate for the Earth's axial rotation, allows the observer to concentrate on the essential work, namely looking at the subject in his field of vision. For large instruments earth-clocks are more or less a necessity, while for medium-sized or smaller instruments they are a definite boon. Various types of drive can be used, spring-powered (clockwork), or small electric motors—even weight-driven mechanisms similar to those used on grandfather clocks have been effectively used for the purpose. The clockwork motor from an old gramophone can here be turned to excellent use, if the centrifugal speed governor is in good working order. The even running speed for which they were designed makes their adaptation for astronomical purposes particularly feasible. The original running time of 15 to 20 minutes can be considerably extended with the addition of extra weights to the governor.

A mechanical drive of this sort has the advantage over electric power in that it is independent of the current supply. Despite this there are doubtless many observers who will want to use electric motors to drive their instruments. However appealing a synchro-motor may seem for this purpose, I would suggest that an electric motor whose speed of revolution can be regulated is really far more suitable for the amateur observer. By this I mean an asynchronous motor with a centrifugal governor. It is then possible to make slight changes in the running speed without undue loss of efficiency. Again, electric gramophone motors are extremely practicable for this. Motors of this sort can, for example, be adapted to make 70–100 revolutions per minute. Furthermore the device lends itself especially to following the Sun and Moon.

Perhaps one of the most important items of equipment for any serious observer is a reliable timepiece. This does not mean that one should have a special astronomical clock, with compensated pendulum and so forth. Not only do such clocks require meticulous maintenance, but they go far beyond the normal requirements of the amateur observer. A precision-made pocket-watch is a much better idea altogether. The most expensive type of these, and one which should meet any contingency, is called a chronometer. For the amateur observer a portable time-piece is in any case a much better proposition than one which is fixed. This does not mean that I am in favour of clocks or watches used for astronomical work being carried around; on the contrary, it is important that such instruments should be protected from excessive vibration and changes of temperature. This is really one of the arguments against using wrist-watches, where during the normal course of wear such stimuli cannot be avoided, and as a result some degree of accuracy has to be forfeited.

An exact time-check should always be made prior to an important observation, such as an eclipse or occultation. However, before one decides to use a particular clock for astronomical purposes, one should give it a test run to see precisely how it behaves. A reliable source from which to obtain exactly the right time is, of course, the radio, but for the work which we want to do it is no use waiting just to hear Big Ben strike; what we are after is real accuracy correct to the second. Because very exact time-checks are also required by ships at sea, the B.B.C. broadcasts the 'pips' at certain times during the day. Greenwich Observatory has always been regarded as the 'timekeeping centre' of the world, so here in Britain we are fortunate in that world time is always reckoned in terms of the Greenwich meridian (GMT or UT, universal time). The observatory was established in 1675 primarily for navigational purposes, and timekeeping has always played a major part in its programme. Here are housed extremely accurate clocks which are linked to the radio. The last of the 'six pips' broadcast regularly over the B.B.C. transmitters indicates the correct time, and any errors are so very slight that they may be entirely disregarded. Another point worth remembering is that the interval between successive 'pips' is exactly one second.

Having set the correct time, the clock should next be allowed to run over a period of at least one week; during this time the reading on the clock should be checked each day at the same hour, and the findings noted in a log. Most clocks tend to gain or lose a little over a given period and what we wish to establish is: (*a*) whether the rate of loss or gain per day is steady, and (*b*) the mean loss or gain per day. In this way extremely accurate timings can be ensured, and these will considerably enhance work on transits of the two inferior planets, occultations and eclipses, to name but a few examples.

The items which have so far been listed in this chapter by no means represent the full complement of equipment for a private observatory. Certain aspects of astronomy, such as solar observations, or photometry, can only be carried out successfully with the help of some specialised apparatus. However, let us not be carried away by items of fancy equipment, and so forget one or two things which, though small, are nevertheless fairly important: a protective cap for the telescope, a cap for the main mirror in a reflector, a shelter for the telescope and mount to give protection from the weather, and some sort of case for the eyepieces, filters and prisms and the like.

Some observers nowadays use revolving turret eyepiece holders, similar to those used on ciné-cameras. This enables them to make an easy switch from one power to another while the telescope is in use, but this is something that can be tried out later when all the really important items have been acquired. Too many odds and ends can easily be a hindrance rather than a help. It is best to start only with the bare essentials and then add to these as required.

Almost an essential for every private observatory is a tool kit—hammers, drills, pliers, saws, screwdrivers and so forth. In addition a small quantity of brass, aluminium and PVC sheeting and tubing of various diameters, as well as some plywood, will always be found useful for some project or other. One should also keep handy a selection of nuts and bolts, and a quantity of one of the modern adhesives.

IV

Proving the Instrument

Everyone who possesses a telescope wants to know from the outset what the maximum capabilities of his instrument are. Telescopes, like people, tend to have their own characteristics and idiosyncrasies, and this is a fact that simply has to be recognised. A precise knowledge of the limitations and quality of any optical instrument is an essential requirement for its full and proper use.

Another fact which must always be borne in mind is that to start with there are bound to be one or two technical shortcomings. Obviously there is not the space here to go into all the details of what can and does happen; the following are therefore no more than cursory accounts. Suffice it to say that, despite the most stringent theoretical precautions, the fault will inevitably come out in practice.

In a refractor the object-lens could happen to be slightly off-centre. As a result, the optical axis, object-lens to eyepiece, will be out of true, and thus the image will lie to one side of the focal point, and appear drop-like instead of circular. On large refractors this fault can be overcome by adjusting the set screws which hold the lens in place. Sometimes brass rings or washers are used to put the matter right.

Similarly, in a reflector poor quality of the image is most likely to be due to the mis-alignment of the mirror system. At the same time, if the matter is one of astigmatism, one must decide whether the fault really lies with the instrument, or the eye of the user. Astigmatism can easily be recognised from the fact that while the extrafocal star image is evenly illuminated, it is not circular; instead it appears elliptical, to a greater or lesser degree. To find out whether one should blame the telescope or oneself, one should first of all twist one's head, so that the eye turns about its optical axis; at the same time one should keep watch to see whether the distortion of the image keeps step with this movement; if it does, then the eye is to blame. Next turn the telescope—if this is possible—about its optical axis, keeping the eye in the same position relative to the eyepiece; if the distortion of the image turns with the telescope, then the fault lies with the instrument. Astigmatism in the optics of a telescope is not a nice thing at all, and the best answer is to return the instrument to the makers for correction or exchange. Other irregularities of the shape of the star image outside the focus, such as a small tail (coma), can be due to insufficient acclimatisation of the instrument before observation. Too great a difference of temperature between the telescope and its environs (for instance if the Sun has been shining on the telescope housing during the day, especially in the late evening when the outside air temperature has already dropped) can be offset by opening up the instrument to air for something like an hour before it is to be used. However, if such tailed images persist despite all precautions, then it means that there is probably a fault in the optics, and this is best put right by an expert.

Whatever happens, one should not be too hasty in apportioning the blame to the optical components of the telescope. For one thing, telescopes are not usually thrown together haphazardly, but are fashioned by craftsmen who rely on personal recommendation rather than the power of advertising. It is therefore extremely unlikely that they would let a faulty instrument out of their hands; better by far to make absolutely certain of one's facts. Temperature changes and other atmospheric conditions can easily lead someone who is not experienced in handling a telescope into thinking that something must be wrong with his instrument. In a reflector the material of which the tube is constructed has a considerable bearing on the quality of the image. In Germany, Robert Wehn has done some research into this problem: 'In order to gain some first-hand experience I mounted a 15 cm reflector on a 16 cm refractor ($5\frac{7}{8}$ and $6\frac{1}{4}$ inches respectively) and systematically observed the same objects through both instruments, working under a spacious dome. We found that in each case the definition of the refractor was the better when the atmosphere was turbulent. Inside the dome it did not matter whether we used a closed or open tube, a wooden or metal one. Under quiet atmospheric conditions the images produced by either instrument were of equal quality. However, in the open different results were obtained. Here radiation from the ground, from the material of the tube itself, and movements of the air all seemed to affect the quality of the image adversely. Least successful was the open tube; using a closed metal tube one could already begin to detect an improvement in the extra-focal image of a star; however, so soon as one inserted a wooden lining into the tube the optimum was attained. Ellison in Armagh informed me that he had found the same thing; he favoured the use of mahogany tubes. The English astronomer, Webb, even went so far as to insulate his tube

47

with asbestos to prevent any interference from body heat. It is an advantage if the diameter of the tube is a few centimetres larger than the diameter of the mirror; probably because the descending cold air tends to cling to the tube.'* From this account we can readily see what an important rôle the material of the tube plays in the case of a reflector, since directly or indirectly it can influence the quality of the image.

As is only to be expected, the appearance of a star in the telescope gives us our first information regarding the quality of the instrument. Assuming that all the conditions (air, optics and observer) are ideal, the image of the star should appear, when in focus, as an absolutely clear and sharp point of light, with no irregularities. If one now slides the eyepiece holder in or out a little way, the image should turn into a series of concentric rings, distending gradually as the eyepiece slides out of focus, but still retaining the shape of a true circle. It is unlikely that all the necessary conditions will be absolutely perfect at the first attempt, or even the second. It is therefore advisable not to reach any conclusion except after extensive trials on a number of different nights. One should always move from the assumption that before any optical components are built into a telescope they will have been thoroughly tested; even if they are home-made, or rather home-ground, there are still plenty of methods for proving the lenses or mirrors. Those who use optics fashioned by themselves will in any case already be conversant with the various tests.

It is not very difficult to test an object-lens for chromatic correction through direct observation of a star. Yellow

* From *Die Sterne*, 1959, Heft 5/6, p. 114.

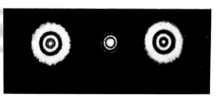

Appearance of a star image in a perfect telescope: from left to right, intra-focal, focal and extra-focal.

Elliptical rings indicate astigmatism, if the major axis of the ellipses rotates through 90 degrees when adjusting from intra-focal to extra-focal.

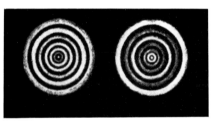

Examples of zone faults in the optics. The distribution of light at intra- and extra-focal setting is not even.

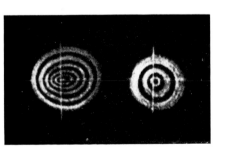

Faulty alignment. Oval distortion with the greater intensity of light at the narrower end.

VII. Correct and faulty images.

D. Lichtenknecker

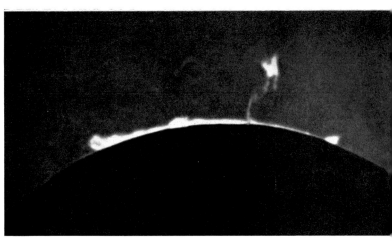

VIII. Prominences at the east limb of the Sun photographed, with a prominence telescope, by R. Brandt, Sonneberg, October 8th 1957, 14 h. G.M.T.

IX. Photograph of full Moon taken by an amateur. 4″ reflector, $f = 176$ cm., yellow filter, $1/25$ sec. exposure. The photographer was Heinrich Trautner, Neustadt near Coburg. The bright rays can be seen well.

and violet light rays make up the secondary spectrum; this can be seen during observation as a coloured ring surrounding bright objects, i.e. the image of a star. To find out if a lens has the required chromatic correction, that is to say whether the lens gathers to one point the right wavelengths, one must observe the star in three aspects and look closely at the colouring of the rim of the image. The following table compiled by D. Lichtenknecker shows the colour of the rim depending on the extent of chromatic correction:

	Extrafocal	*Focal*	*Intrafocal*
1. OBJECT-LENS (visual)			
(a) Over-corrected	orange—chrome yellow	poor image with bluish tinge	blue—violet
(b) Well corrected	green—greenish yellow	sharp image	crimson (aniline purple)
(c) Under-corrected	blue–green	poor image with reddish tinge	reddish yellow
2. OBJECT-LENS (photo.)			
Well corrected	intense blue–green	poor image strong reddish tinge	brick red—red lead

Despite the apparent simplicity of this test, it is nevertheless accurate and fully adequate for the needs of amateur observers.

Two further criteria for judging the quality of the optics of a telescope are its 'resolving power' and 'light-gathering power'. There are ways and means of testing both these through practical observation.

When we try to assess the *resolution* of a telescope, we have to take into account that there are two distinct types of telescopic subjects. In the first place there are those

4* 49

which show illuminated discs on which certain darker features may be discerned (Sun, Moon and planets); in the second, those which can be seen as pinpoints of light against the black background of the sky (stars). Just how comparable results obtained in these two groups are is open to argument. Obviously conditions have to be more favourable during observations of, say, planets than they do for looking at double stars. Professional and amateur astronomers alike have been engaged in heated discussions as to why this should be so. Periodicals in the United States published the results of large-scale experiments to prove the point. I personally regard such model experiments with a certain amount of scepticism. Some of the results claimed were so fantastic that one might be forgiven for wondering why so many observers spend their money on four- or six-inch telescopes, when it would seem that they could achieve equivalent results with instruments measuring no more than three-quarters of an inch in diameter. Such tests really only confute themselves. In every instance both the theoretical, as well as the practical, difference between the resolving power of the two types of subject will not be very considerable. So far as larger telescopes are concerned, any discussion regarding the theoretical resolution is of academic interest only, since the turbulence and turbidity of the atmosphere, particularly in the vicinity of urban areas, soon place an effective limit on any possible performance.

If, on looking through the eyepiece, stellar images never actually appear as absolutely perfect points of light, then this is not only an effect of the atmosphere, but also to a slight distortion of the light rays which in a refractor occurs at the edge of the object-lens, while in a reflector the edge of the mirror has the same effect. As a result perfect points of light are magnified into tiny discs of star-light even in the best possible atmospheric conditions. In a refractor the situation is further aggravated through the presence of the secondary spectrum. But the owners of reflecting telescopes should not start congratulating them-selves too early on their wisdom in choosing this type of instrument. In the optical system of the reflector the main mirror has its own subtle ways of distorting the light rays which reach it. The 'stellar discs' diminish with in-creasing aperture, but even at best all star images are only approximately point-like, and as the magnification increases the disc shape becomes more and more ap-parent, as well as several concentric diffraction rings, even though the instrument is in perfect focus. In a two-inch telescope this change from point to disc shape of the stellar image can be noticed—assuming optical per-fection—from a magnification of about × 100; in a four-inch instrument from about × 180.

The above is of interest when one comes to test a tele-scope, and can best be demonstrated by means of double-star observations. The distance between the two com-ponents of a double varies from pair to pair, and, according to the aperture of the telescope, will either permit separation—so that one can see two distinct star images—or despite all magnification still appear only as one light source. Between these two extremes there are a number of transition stages; but if the aperture of the telescope is too small to resolve a particular double, then the true nature of the latter will not be revealed to the observer.

The theoretical limits at which double stars can just be separated at certain specific telescope apertures can be worked out from the formula: $11''/d =$ separation limit in seconds of arc.* Here '*d*' is the effective diameter in centimetres. With this rule of thumb any amateur observer can calculate the theoretical limits of his instrument if the aperture ratio lies between 1:10 and 1:20. The only other consideration is that both components of the double should have more or less the same apparent magnitude, i.e. brightness. Stars which are appreciably brighter than others will also show greater diffraction effects (with high powers such as are required to determine limits in double star observations), and so tend to swamp the diffraction effects of their fainter companions. The following table gives some useful comparisons for the separation of double stars:

APERTURE OF TELESCOPE	50 mm (2 in.)	80 mm (3 in.)	110 mm (4·3 in.)	150 mm (6 in.)
DISTANCE BETWEEN STARS (sec. of arc)	2·3	1·8	1·0	0·8

The planets form the classic tests for the resolution of dark details on light backgrounds, and the planet Jupiter seems to be the subject most favoured by astronomers. Instruments of two or three inches diameter should, with magnifications of × 80 to × 100, show the more prominent dark and light bands quite easily. Using similar magnification a four-inch telescope should enable one to make out the shadows of Jupiter's satellites on the surface of the planet. The Cassini division in the ring system of the planet Saturn constitutes yet another test for three- or four-inch telescopes, but, of course, the angle at which the rings happen to be placed has to be taken into account. When the white pole caps on Mars

* The symbol ″ in this context should not be confused with that for the *inch*, but denotes 3,600ths of a degree, i.e. *second* of arc.

are at their greatest extent, one should be able to see them with a two-inch telescope, but in order to detect finer detail on the surface of the Red Planet an instrument with a diameter of at least four inches (100 mm) is needed.

In contrast to the observations of double stars, it is here better not to use an eyepiece of too high a power. As a rough guide, the magnification should be about × 30 to × 50 per inch diameter to obtain optimum efficiency. Another difference between the two types of observation is that atmospheric turbulence tends to influence the observation of the planets to a greater extent than it does the separation of double stars.

The light-gathering power of an astronomical telescope can be assessed in terms of the faintest star which that particular telescope is just able to pick up. The apparent brightnesses of stars are classified according to a scale of magnitudes, where the difference between successive magnitudes is the logarithmic function. It is generally reckoned that the faintest star which can just be seen with the naked eye has an apparent magnitude of 6, often expressed as 6^m. However, need it be said, that anyone who attempts to see a star of this magnitude from somewhere like the middle of Piccadilly Circus in London, or Broadway, New York, is doomed to failure from the outset! This is not because city-dwellers are considered to have worse eyesight than their country cousins, but because the illuminations of any urban area (street lighting, advertisements and so forth) cast far too much stray light. Thus any experiments to determine the light-gathering power of a telescope should, and indeed must, take place on a clear, dark night, when there is no Moon, and as far as possible from sodium vapour lamps and other sources of stray light.

Proving the Instrument

In order to establish the limit for a particular instrument, we choose a star field containing a generous sprinkling of fairly bright stars (not brighter than 5^m). From then on the process is reasonably simple. The stars observed in the field are checked against a star chart, and the identities recorded. All that is then necessary is to look up their apparent magnitudes in a star catalogue, and the rest is obvious. Pickering's method of determining the light-gathering power of a telescope by means of the North Polar Sequence has become widely used. All the stars in this test region lie in the vicinity of the north celestial pole, and so are visible from our latitude all the year round.*

Except for the resolution test on double stars, we usually use only low-power eyepieces for purely stellar observations. This is not only because such eyepieces offer us a considerably wider field of vision, but also because increasing the magnification does not reveal any stars fainter than those which would otherwise be visible; for one thing, the higher magnification causes the points of starlight to distend into disc shapes due to the diffraction effect, as a result of which any fainter objects are swamped. This, at any rate, is the theory. In practice it turns out that, as a result of the darkening of the black

* Particularly recommended for amateurs are two star atlases and the catalogues that go with them:

The *Bonner Durchmusterung* (Dümmler, Bonn) consists of two catalogue volumes and 64 charts showing the positions and magnitudes of 457,857 stars lying between the north celestial pole and 23 degrees southerly declination; it includes stars down to magnitude 9·5 apparent brightness.

Atlas Coeli by A. Bečvář (Prague), consists of 16 charts and one catalogue volume; it lists stars down to magnitude 7·75.

Another excellent atlas for amateur observers is *Norton's Star Atlas* compiled by A. P. Norton and published by Gall & Inglis.

background, a higher power does in fact facilitate the perception of fainter points of light. Magnification of the diffraction effect makes hardly any difference near the limit of vision, for, when it comes to such minute and faint objects, the resolving power of the eye is not sufficiently discriminating.

Nevertheless, the best thing at first is to carry out the test so far as is practicable with a small power, something between about ×20 and ×80. Only after sufficient experience has been gained is it advisable for the amateur observer to embark upon experiments with higher magnifications, to find out what 'marginal' stars he can discern.

The difference between the limit of vision of the instrument and the naked eye in terms of magnitudes gives us a measure for the efficiency of the telescope. For this purpose the limit of visibility is defined as comprising those stars which are only just fleetingly distinguishable—when one first glimpses the star one is not quite sure whether one really has seen something or not, and several attempts are usually necessary to make absolutely certain. Moving from the assumption that the limit of visibility for the naked eye is 6^m, one can expect the following limits for telescopes:

Diameter		Refractor	Reflector
(in.)	(mm)	$(^m)$	$(^m)$
2	54	11·0	—
4	108	12·5	12·7
6	162	13·5	13·7
8	216	14·0	14·2

The values shown in the table are, of course, no more than a rough guide and should therefore not be taken too literally. Reflection and absorption losses in the object

lenses of a refractor, or the secondary mirror in a reflector (except with the Neo-Brachyt design), can have
varying effects, quite apart from the ever-changing
meteorological and environmental conditions.

It is quite a well-known fact that certain drugs can
render the human eye more receptive of faint stimuli.
An increase in the hormones which affect sight (vitamin
A), increases also the immediate, as well as the ultimate,
adaptability of the eye. Thus the receptive power of the
eye can be temporarily improved to the extent that stars
between $0·5^m$ and $1·0^m$ beyond the theoretical limit can,
in fact, be seen. This demonstrates to what extent a
number of physiological factors can influence where the
so-called limit lies.

One kind of instrument, especially developed for its
high light-gathering ability, is known as a 'comet-seeker'.
As the name implies, such instruments are used in the
search for comets, which are generally very faint objects
indeed. The instruments have a wide field of vision with
sharp definition, and their aperture ratios lie somewhere
between $1:6$ to $1:8$. However, such instruments are not
made for high magnifications, and their price is a matter
which is better not discussed. So far as the ordinary
amateur is concerned, a good pair of binoculars can
successfully be used to hunt for comets. Alternatively one
can use a small monocular telescope such as is used to
observe artificial Earth satellites. These instruments have
an aperture of about 2 inches, a power of $\times 6$ or $\times 7$, and
a field of vision of about 12 degrees.

In the normal course of events, the amateur will
scarcely if ever have occasion to observe stars whose
magnitudes lie at the limit of which his telescope is capable. Nevertheless, a knowledge of the limiting magnitude

56

is an essential precept for assessing the quality, or making full use, of a particular telescope.

Quite apart from testing the instrument in the first place, it is vitally important to look after it carefully, if best results are to be obtained. Dust is one of the principal bugbears, and in the course of time some is bound to settle on the main lens or mirror. On no account should this be simply *wiped* off, for even the smallest particle of grit can scratch the surface, particularly in the case of a mirror. Any dust on the optical surfaces should be removed carefully with a soft brush, and brushes for this purpose can be purchased at any photographic dealer— some even incorporate a small blower. If desired, the final polishing of a lens may be carried out with a soft leather, but on no account should a mirror be treated in this manner, and if the lens is of the coated, or bloomed, type, it should, after dusting, be cleaned only with a wad of cotton wool soaked in alcohol.

The exposed—i.e. unpainted—metal surfaces on the telescope and mount should be greased from time to time. This is to prevent corrosion. In addition, the bearings of the axes should be kept well greased to ensure their smooth running.

V

Learning to See

In the process of putting his telescope through its paces, the amateur astronomer at once comes up against the actual business of observing. To start with he is bound to feel slightly disappointed with what he sees. One reason for this is that most of us approach a telescope for the first time with a preconceived idea of what it will show us, and most of the bodies on which we then train the telescope fail to measure up to our expectations. The only subjects which are perhaps what we had imagined them are the Sun and the Moon. Thus the first look through an astronomical telescope is something of an 'optical awakening'.

Anyone who wishes to drive a car has to have a licence, and even then it still does not mean that he knows how to drive—but only that he may. In many ways, this is analogous to the enthusiast who has just acquired a telescope, knows all about it technically, and even has a fair general astronomical knowledge. All these facts still do not mean that he really knows how to observe. Thorough and reliable observation through a telescope has to be learned and requires a fair amount of painstaking practice. This is one of the reasons why anyone just starting out along the long road of practical astronomy will be well advised to restrict himself at first to a fairly modest instrument, and not allow himself to

Learning to See

become side-tracked by all sorts of gadgets. The experience gathered at the eyepiece of a small telescope will pay off well in later years, when one might aspire to a six- or eight-inch instrument. In any case a small instrument will reduce the initial frustration and disappointment.

Even a giant telescope can only partially bridge the immensity of the universe. It is the astronomer's most important tool, absolutely essential to his work; but it must be realised that, however good it may be, it too is limited. This applies even more to the amateur observer, whose instrument is relatively much smaller than that of the professional. Although, as has just been stated, the telescope is important, the eye of the observer himself probably plays an even greater rôle. Our eyes provide us with a dimensional impression of our environment, and with certain reservations they should perform the same function in telescopic observation. Admittedly this is not at all easy at first, since observation through a telescope is carried out with one eye only. So, what do we do with the other? The beginner usually closes the eye not in use, or covers it with one hand.

There are, of course, devices allowing binocular observation through a telescope; but, owing to their high cost and the inevitable loss of light they entail, they are rarely met with. Binoculars, or field glasses, are a well-known exception, and these lend themselves for use as compact astronomical instruments, but their application is necessarily very limited. Heinz von Seggern, an amateur in Bremen, Germany has constructed his own binocular telescope (Plate XXII). This consists of two identical spherical mirrors 7 cm (2⅝ in.) diameter ($f=1:12$) mounted parallel. Above the two 'flats' there

59

are two rotatable drums containing reversing prisms from a pair of field-glasses. The eyepiece sleeves are fixed eccentrically to the drums, corresponding to the deflection of the light ray by the prisms. This arrangement allows the eyepieces to be brought into the correct alignment for the particular observer. Von Seggern made the whole thing himself, including the grinding of the two main mirrors. This is one way of providing oneself with an instrument bigger than conventional field-glasses at a reasonable price. Basically we have here a typical binocular system: two eyepieces and two objectives. Moreover, there is no loss of light such as is the case where binocular eyepieces are used with only one objective.

The first essential before trying to make any observation is to allow one's eyes to become accustomed to the dark. Particularly faint objects such as comets and spiral nebulæ demand an even longer acclimatisation period before one starts work, and this also applies to testing for light-gathering power. On the other hand, bright subjects showing discs, such as the Moon and some of the planets, quite apart from the Sun (which can only be observed indirectly, or by means of special safety devices), do not necessarily produce better observational results. Here the light may easily be so bright as to swamp the eye of the observer. All the devices designed to shield the eye from such glare, however, invariably also reduce the ability to discern some of the finer details.

So far as the planets Mars, Venus and Jupiter are concerned, the glare can to some extent be counteracted by increasing the magnification, but here it must be remembered that for a number of reasons the power of the eyepiece cannot simply be stepped up *ad infinitum*.

Learning to See

In lunar observation it is best, for example, to choose a time before or after the Moon is full—moreover, the shadows are more prominent then; failing that, to observe when the background of the sky is still relatively light. In this way the observation will not be spoilt by an excess of light, nor the eye of the observer tired unduly.

A rapid switch from one type of telescopic subject to another, say, something like fifteen minutes of looking at the Moon and then searching for a difficult double star, is an unsatisfactory way for anyone to set about observing. For one thing the difference between the two types of subject is eminently likely to strain the eye. It is far better to restrict viewing to one or two definite objectives; this helps to make the actual observing far more pleasant, and is also a step in the right direction towards serious and systematic astronomical observation. Moreover, it will enable the observer to gather the necessary personal experience in handling his telescope.

The observer's physical condition, and the environment in which the observation is made, also exercise an influence which must not be underestimated. Any form of exhaustion through hard physical work, or nervous tension during the day, is soon transmitted to the eye, and hunger or drowsiness will also affect the alertness of the observer. If one is accustomed to wearing glasses, it is better not to use these for looking through the telescope. The normal visual faults such as long or short sight, can easily be compensated for by a twist of the eyepiece focusing screw. The observation loses nothing by this manœuvre, and spectacles are in any case a positive nuisance when working at the telescope, forcing the observer to hold his eye too far from the eyepiece; not only that, but there is also always the danger of a certain amount of reflection from the spectacle lens, an effect which can play havoc with the observation.

Sometimes feeble features on the threshold of perception can be seen more easily if they are brought slightly nearer the edge of the field of vision in the telescope. However, this is only a dodge intended merely to get over an immediate difficulty, and, like all dodges, should never be made the regular form of procedure. It can be helpful in certain instances, but should be avoided if possible. On the other hand, it is on the whole better not to look directly at the object under observation, but slightly to one side of it. This is not for the purpose of taking this object by surprise, but has to do with the sensitivity of the retina of the eye. If it is found that there is a marked difference in definition between the centre and the edge of the field of vision, even though the instrument is not being pushed beyond its maximum, then the optical system of the telescope, or the eyes of the observer, should be given a thorough check.

It goes without saying that optical and mechanical perfection are both absolutely essential factors for pleasant observing. A rickety stand, or excessive play in the eyepiece slider, or a jerky slow-motion drive, to mention some of the more obvious faults that can occur, are able to ruin what might have been a very pleasant night's observing; the results achieved are unlikely to be of much value, and, if the situation is allowed to persist, the utter frustration might induce the telescope user to do something nasty to his tormentor. Far better to try to remedy the cause before one's nerves are entirely frayed, for the would-be astronomer has quite enough to contend with in the whims of the weather. Cloud conditions can often alter dramatically in the few critical moments before or during an observation.

From the purely technical aspect, telescopic observation is dependent for success on three factors: the observer, the instrument and weather conditions. The art of observing is really no more than the optimum coincidence of all three factors, but a great deal of personal experience and an appreciable apprenticeship are required if one is to make anything of the opportunities when they arise. It is as well for anyone just beginning to observe to realise that even observers of long standing continuously improve their techniques as they work. This is one of the challenges of amateur astronomy.

VI

Starting to Observe

There is a danger that what sets out to become a home observatory turns into something which is really no more than a workshop for things astronomical. Sooner or later every amateur has to decide to which field of observation he will devote his principal efforts. As with all other branches of science, astronomy can become instructive and rewarding for the layman only if he sets himself to perform a particular task in a systematic manner, no matter how restricted it may have to be. Just looking at the stars and planets is all right so far as it goes, and gives many people some enjoyable hours, but it really does not go quite far enough. For the serious amateur this stage should be no more than a stepping-stone to something much grander; he wants to enlarge his knowledge, and his personal observations should help him in this.

The important thing to bear in mind is that any astronomical observation should always aim to fulfil at least one of the following conditions:

1. Satisfy a particular æsthetic interest of the observer;
2. Provide some specific data;
3. Form a part of some particular programme of observation.

There is a reason for each of these three points. In

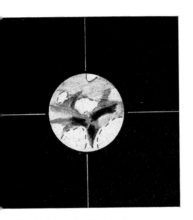

Red filter RG2 (Schott)

Green filter VG6 (Schott)

Blue filter BG12 (Schott)

X. Mars 1956. Examples of visual observation using filters.
Observations by the author—September 5th.

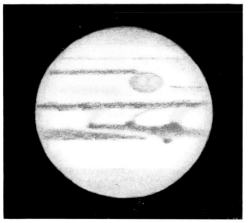

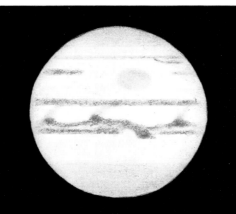

XI. Jupiter 1961. Showing change in position of the Great Red Spot (*above*) August 2nd centre 3°, (*below*) September 10th 7° in System I. Observer E. Antoniadi, Geneva.

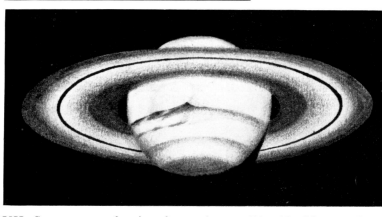

XII. Saturn 1955, showing the rarely seen Ring D. Observer R. M. Baum, Chester, May 29th 1955 22 h. 35 m. G.M.T. 4½″ refractor, × 180

amateur astronomical work the main considerations are always likely to be either æsthetic or educational. An amateur is rarely, if ever, able to undertake a task which is purely scientific in its nature. The main point is that, whatever programme an amateur does undertake, he should approach this in a scientific manner.

Every programme of observation, if it is to be carried out systematically, requires sketches of what has been observed. A pile of drawings on odd scraps of paper that happened to come to hand is far from being the best way of setting about this problem. The only really satisfactory method is to keep a log in which to enter the observations made. Quite apart from a written account of the actual observation, there are one or two pertinent facts which should also be entered. First there must be a description of the instrument under the headings: (*a*) diameter, (*b*) type, (*c*) mount; then a description of the place of observation (i.e. its geographic latitude and longitude as precisely as possible); and lastly the name of the observer. All this information can be shown at the beginning of the log, and need not be repeated except when beginning a new book, or if any of the circumstances have changed. Some items of information, however, must be given for each observation entered: the date, the time, the atmospheric conditions and the power of the eyepiece used. Only if all these facts are known can any individual observation be evaluated in its proper perspective. Incidentally, when writing the date, it is just as well to name the day of the week as well as putting the day of the month, as this provides an additional check. Usually the year is written first, next comes the name of the month, then the day of the month, and last the day of the week. It is as well always to make a habit of quoting the time of day in GMT; not only is this universally accepted and understood, but it also avoids any confusion about British Summer Time, which may vary from year to year. A description of the seeing conditions, on the other hand, does pose a bit of a problem, since any estimate in this respect necessarily entails some latitude either way, and the various scales devised to meet the contingency can vary considerably. Yet accuracy is desirable, and, if not absolute accuracy, then consistency, for this is a critical factor in assessing the observational value of the record. It is therefore a good thing to work out a sort of scale starting with 'good', through 'satisfactory', down to 'bad' or 'poor'; such a scale can then be augmented with plus or minus symbols, in order to give a finer definition. It is also necessary to differentiate between the steadiness of the atmosphere and the clarity of the sky. The best method is to make an entry under each of these headings using the same scale. The reason for this is that the air may be quite still, but visibility may still be restricted on account of haze. With a little practice it is surprising how expert one can soon become in assessing the atmospheric conditions. Should one decide to use a scale of numbers for this purpose, it is essential to define the code accurately, and, furthermore, if results are at any time to be sent to another observer, to make sure that he too understands exactly what you mean. Of the two, the former method is probably preferable.

It is important to try to establish some sort of objective assessment as to the quality of the image, so as to have a constant basis for evaluating individual observations. The resolution of double stars is one way of achieving this end; by observing and measuring the distances between the components of a double, measured in seconds, or fractions of a second of arc. The aim is to see how small a distance can be determined on a particular evening's viewing. In the U.S.A. Clyde Tombaugh and B. A. Smith have developed a picture quality scale along these lines:

Quality Scale	*Image Diameter* (=*Distance apart of double*)
−4	50″ (seconds of arc)
−3	32″
−2	20″
−1	12·6″
0	7·9″
+1	5·0″
+2	3·2″
+3	2·0″
+4	1·3″
+5	0·79″
+6	0·5″
+7	0·32″
+8	0·2″
+9	0·13″

If the same doubles are to be used on numerous occasions, it is essential to check if the distance between the components of each pair remains constant, or whether it varies over a given period.

Obviously any additional apparatus used, or alterations to the instrument, must be shown in the observational data.

It is not possible in this small volume to list all the subjects which are suitable for observation. I have therefore had to restrict myself to some suggestions rather than detailed descriptions. In any case the relevant information is always available in books devoted to a particular aspect of astronomy. Some of the more important books are named in the bibliography.

VII

Observing the Sun

Pride of place in any guide to observation is usually reserved for the Sun. The amateur just starting out to observe is also likely to make this body his first objective. This is not at all a bad idea, for a great deal of useful work can be done with a relatively small instrument. Another point in its favour is that one does not have to sacrifice any sleep in order to carry out one's observations.

However, as has already been pointed out, it is extremely dangerous to look directly at the Sun unless *adequate* shielding is used. It is not advisable to gaze too long at the Sun with the naked eye, let alone through binoculars or a telescope. Most of us at some time or another have played about with a magnifying glass in the Sun, focusing the latter's rays on to some object until it begins to scorch. Not only does one collect all the light rays at the focus of the lens, but one concentrates the heat as well. From this the peril of looking at the Sun through a telescope should be obvious without further explanation. The indirect method of observation, on the other hand, is always absolutely safe, since the image of the Sun is projected on to a screen, and not on to the eye.

The practice of placing filters into the optical system is not really to be recommended. Such filters are usually fitted between the collecting (convex) and the eye lens, but they can also be placed after the eye lens (i.e. immediately before the eye of the observer). The main danger lies in the fact that the heat is quite likely to cause the filter glass to crack, so that in the latter instance there is a chance of a stray splinter of glass damaging the eye. The other disadvantage is that the image seen in the telescope will always be tinged with the colour of the filter. By reducing the aperture of the telescope to something like 2 inches (50 mm) one can reduce the risk of the filter being shattered, but this can only be done at the expense of definition.

A much better proposition for making direct observation of the Sun is a specially designed solar viewer. A pentaprism or solar diagonal, or even just a system of mirrors, deflects the sunlight so that a great deal of the glare is absorbed, and in some designs much of the heat is

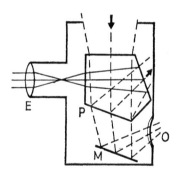

Fig. 7. Light rays in a solar pentaprism.
P = prism, M = mirror, O = opening, E = eyepiece.

The light which escapes at the first reflection falls on to a metal mirror and is radiated away through an aperture. The light energy from the second reflection in the prism is rendered ineffective by the matt black surface and a grey filter in the eyepiece dims the light still further.

also dissipated. The image of the Sun which reaches the eyepiece is thus so weakened in intensity that it may be rendered harmless with a slightly grey-tinted filter.

An excellent piece of apparatus for solar observation is what is known as a 'polarising helioscope'. In a most ingenious way the light from the Sun is polarised by means of two pairs of dark mirrors, and a method of reciprocal displacement allows the image of the Sun to be controlled from glaring brilliance to almost complete extinction. The observer is thus able to regulate the instrument to whatever brilliance suits him. Neither is there any kind of discoloration. This device is absolutely ideal for solar observers, and, needless to say, correspondingly expensive. Nevertheless it is just the thing for anyone wishing to specialise in this aspect of astronomy.

Simpler, cheaper, and yet absolutely without any risk at all is the method of solar projection. Here the image of the Sun appears on a screen fixed at a convenient distance from the eyepiece; the optimum distance at which the screen should be placed is best determined by trial and error. Once this distance has been found it is reasonably easy to construct some sort of holder which can be clamped to the instrument and which will then hold the screen steady at that distance. Except on a Newtonian reflector, it is as well also to rig up some sort of shield which will cast a shadow on the vital region of the screen; it need only be a piece of hardboard or plywood with a hole cut out of its middle just big enough to slide on to the eyepiece draw tube. Here again, necessity is the mother of invention, and a little thought on the problem will soon show what is wanted. The projection method also has other advantages. In the first place, a sheet of graph paper can be clipped on to the screen—the outline of the solar disc can be drawn on this beforehand—then any sunspots may be marked in with complete accuracy and any shift in position from one day to the next becomes immediately apparent. The method is also ideal for demonstration purposes, since a number of observers can see the projected image simultaneously. This is particularly useful when members of one's family and friends want to see some phenomenon such as an eclipse of the Sun.

It is also possible to attach a 120-degree prism to the eyepiece, which on some types of telescope makes for greater comfort during observation, but otherwise is not really a vitally important feature. What is important, however, is that the supports for the screen should be sufficiently rigid to prevent it wobbling about, yet at the same time the structure should not be so heavy that it destroys the stability of the instrument, nor yet consist of so many supporting rods that side viewing becomes difficult.

One of the principal tasks of solar observation is the recording and plotting of sunspots. Because conditions for observing the Sun are so very favourable, this body enjoys virtually no privacy at all these days. There are a great many solar observers in all parts of the globe, and it is probably true to say that there is not a single moment of any day when someone, somewhere, is not keeping a watch on the Sun. Thus any observations made by amateurs have to be of extremely high quality if they are intended as contributions towards an overall programme of observation. If an amateur can qualify for this, then his work will take on a new significance, for one of his observations could well turn out to be all that is necessary to fill some particular gap in our knowledge. Even if one's work is not carried out as part of some wider programme of research, the keeping of statistics on sunspot activity over a long period, and a study of the characteristics of individual sunspots, can be extremely interesting in its own right.

It must not be thought that there is no work to be done involving the observation of fine detail. Apart from studying the structure of sunspots, there are also such phenomena as faculæ, the light net-like veins on the surface of the Sun, and granulation, an appearance of graininess, where lighter-coloured spots cover the whole face of the Sun, like a sort of rash. All these phenomena provide plenty of opportunity of observing fine details. Prominences can be rendered visible by means of special spectroscopes built for this purpose; or one can use a prominence telescope of the kind constructed by Professor Otto Nögel, of Landshut in Germany.

The prominence telescope is an extremely ingenious instrument which allows us to see these huge incandescent tongues leaping out from the limb of the Sun's disc. Normally the glaring expanse of the face of the Sun completely swamps these phenomena. This instrument, which is constructed on the principle of Lyot's coronagraph, obscures the main disc of the Sun and shuts out much of the scattered light surrounding it, thus affording us a view of the limb only.

Not only is this device ingenious, but it is also one which can be built by an amateur; however, the work is precise and the parts cannot simply be thrown together in a couple of hours or so. For those who are interested, the instructions are as follows:

The main structure consists of four light metal discs each 4–5 mm thick (5/32–13/64 in.) connected together by three sets of four rods (see diagram). The optical parts are fitted into holes in the centres of the four discs, S1 to S4, as shown.

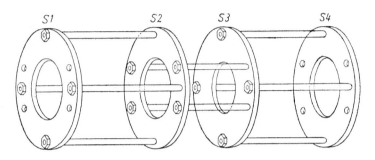

Fig. 8. Frame for holding optical parts for Nögel's prominence telescope.

Each of the discs has holes drilled into it to carry the spacing rods; these in turn have screw threads at either end and are secured to the discs by means of two nuts. The distances between successive discs, and hence also the lengths of each set of spacing rods, are dictated by the optical parts used. Thus the space between S1 and S2 is such that the object-lens in S1 brings the image of the Sun into sharp focus on the blanking-off cone in S2, while S3 and S4 are so placed that a second object-lens in S3 brings the blanking-off cone into sharp focus either on the plane of the film, or the focal plane of the eyepiece.

Nögel suggests the following: if the first object-lens has a focal length of 54 cm, the distance between S1 and S2 is then equal to 54 cm less the amount by which the object-lens, mounted in its sleeve, protrudes in front of S1; if the image of the Sun, which in this case is about 5 mm diameter and the same as that of the blanking-off cone, is to be enlarged to a diameter of 10 mm in the film plane, the distance between S2 and S3 has to be 1·5 times the focal length of the second object-lens (S3); and the distance between S3 and S4 must be such that the distance from S3 to the film plane, or the focal plane of the eyepiece, is three times the focal lens of the second object-lens. In other words, if the latter is a small objective from

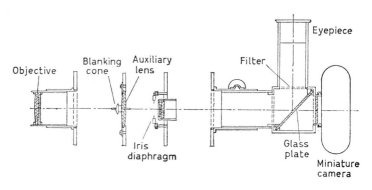

Fig. 9. Diagram of Nögel's prominence telescope.

a pair of field glasses with a focal length of 15 cm, S2–S3 = 225 mm, and S3–S4 = 450 mm, *less* the length of the eyepiece draw tube, measured to the plane of the eyepiece diaphragm, or the film plane.

The hole cut in the centre of S1 is threaded, and a sleeve screwed into it. A draw tube with the object-lens fits into this sleeve. This arrangement permits easy focusing of the Sun's image on the blanking-off cone.

The aperture at the centre of S2 is slightly recessed to hold an auxiliary lens, whose function is to provide a base for the blanking-off cone. A hole is drilled in the centre of the lens, and using lead-oxide–glycerine cement a pin or peg is then bedded into this; blanking-off cones of various diameters may then be pushed on to the pin, as required. The auxiliary lens is an ordinary biconvex spectacle lens with a diameter of 30–40 mm. For the particular model being described, the focal length should lie between 150 and 160 mm (6·5 diopters).

An iris type diaphragm is held a short distance from S3 by means of three long screws, which in turn are held in S3 by lock nuts, so that it is possible to adjust the length of the screws and thus place the diaphragm in exactly the right position. The iris diaphragm should come just where the image of the object-lens mounting is projected through the auxiliary lens. Incidentally, such iris diaphragms can be found in old cameras.

S4, like S1, holds a draw tube, and here also a part from an old slide projector can come in useful. A cube fashioned from sheet metal, though plywood will do, is attached to the end of the draw tube. On the side of the cube opposite the draw tube is the camera—35 mm for preference—with its lens removed. The sleeve for the control eyepiece draw tube is fitted to another of the sides of the cube. One of the sides of the cube should be removable, making a hatch to allow access to a glass plate secured to the interior of the cube by pieces of cork. The glass should be inserted at an angle of 45 degrees so as to reflect the light rays into the eyepiece. It is as well to arrange for the two threads, eyepiece sleeve and camera, to be similar. In this way the eyepiece can replace the camera for visual observation.

Filters are required; these should be deep red (e.g. Schott RG2) which will almost completely filter off the visible light ranging from a wavelength of 6300 towards the yellow. Also excellent for this purpose are interference filters—7–9 mμ are perfectly adequate. Messrs Schott of Mainz, for instance, supply such a filter by

Dr. Geffcken; the diameter is 25 mm, and it is good value for money.

So much for the actual description of the 'works' of Nögel's prominence telescope. The whole thing now has to be fitted into a tube with hatches to allow access to the various optical parts which might need adjustment. It is, however, advisable to acquire the tube first and then to build the above structure to fit into it; otherwise one could well waste a great deal of time looking for a tube which is just the right size. Those who do not feel sufficiently competent to construct an instrument of this kind could have the discs and rods made to specification by a small engineering firm and then try to interest a local optician in the project. The effort will be worth while, for this really is a very fine instrument for anybody who intends making a serious study of the Sun.

Next let us deal with the subject of making drawings of sunspots.

In the first place it is advisable to make a stencil which can be used for drawing the outline shape of the Sun. The outline shape should be divided into four quadrants by right-angled axes, corresponding to a view of the Sun through an eyepiece with cross sights. At the commencement of observation, one adjusts the horizontal hair-line so that a given sunspot will move along parallel to it for a fairly long time if one keeps the telescope static. The division of the apparent solar disc into four quadrants makes the accurate placing of single, or groups of sunspots relatively easy. From the purely statistical aspect one need not bother about what the individual sunspots look like, but accurate reproductions of their appearance will, of course, enhance one's observations. It is best to draw the sunspot in pencil; the tracery of the faculæ can then be depicted in red crayon and any granulation in green.

The Swiss solar observer Prof. Waldmeier of Zürich has classified the important types of spot formations into nine groups. This scale can be augmented and extended as required. (See Fig. 10.)

A record of sunspot groups is important, since solar activity is expressed by the relative number of sunspots ($=R$). If we know the number of groups g, and the number of individual spots f, we can calculate R by means of the formula:

$$R = k(10g + f)$$

The factor k can be ignored so far as we are concerned; its purpose is really only to even out the results obtained with telescopes of divers diameters, so that there can be some basis for comparison. The astronomer R. Wolf worked on the assumption that $k=1$ for instruments of 8 cm (3 in.) diameter. If the aperture is smaller, then k should be greater than 1; if larger then k is less then 1. As their name implies, the R numbers are no more than relative, and can only be considered to carry weight if they are the result of a great many observations. The observatory of the Swiss Federation in Zürich is also the international centre for solar observation, where all the data are collected, and correlated.

Any individual spot usually consists of a core (umbra) and a surrounding ring (penumbra). The position of the umbra within the penumbra makes an interesting study requiring observation of fine detail. Towards the limb of the Sun's disc, the core of the sunspot can appear rather more eccentrically placed in the penumbra than one might expect. Sometimes such a phenomenon is observ-

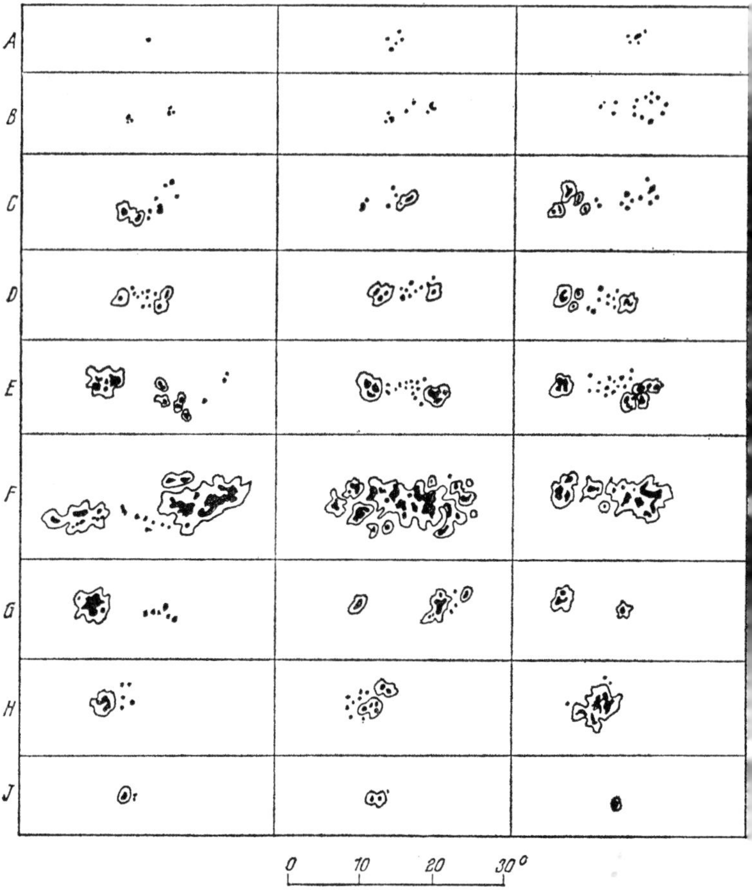

Fig. 10. Development of Sunspot Groups.

The development of typical spot-groups is shown from left to right.

A: Very small group, at the limit of visibility, consisting originally of a single small umbra which never develops to large size.

B: Small two-spot group, never large, and which finally breaks up into a collection of small umbræ.

C: Small to moderate group, visible with a 3-inch refractor, in which some spots develop penumbræ.

D: Moderate two-spot group, in which both the preceding and following spots attain some size.

E: Large group, containing complex spots with penumbræ.

F: Very large group, perhaps attaining naked-eye visibility, with giant complex spots which are difficult to draw accurately because they contain so much detail.

G: Group in which the preceding spot develops first, while the following spot appears later and disappears earlier.

H: Group consisting basically of one moderate spot, which may however break up.

J: Group consisting of one small spot, with penumbra, which may at times show division.

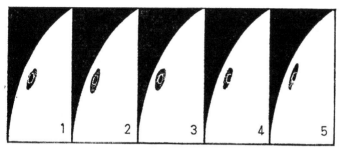

Fig. 11. The Wilson Effect.

...ble when the sunspot is near the east or west limb, but while it is in the vicinity of the meridian the umbra nevertheless appears centrally placed. The phenomenon is known as the Wilson Effect, and can form an interesting part of the observational programme for amateur solar observers.

Mention has already been made of the movement of sunspots parallel to the horizontal hair-line in the eyepiece. This enables us to determine the east–west line with great accuracy, and we can go on from there to find the rotation axis of the Sun; this is inclined at a certain angle from the perpendicular to the line. The exact angle of the solar axis may be looked up in a suitable astronomical almanac. With the aid of a heliographic grid it is then possible to determine the heliographic co-ordinates of the various features, such as sunspots, singly or in groups. Where the projection method of observation is used the whole operation is even simpler. If the co-ordinates are marked on the screen, one merely turns this to find the east–west line and all that remains is to draw in the solar axis.

An aspect of solar observation which offers much prospect is photography. The brilliance of the subject obviates the necessity for long time-exposures, and there is a fairly wide field of choice in the matter of suitable emulsions. However, we shall deal with this topic more fully in a later chapter (see p. 103).

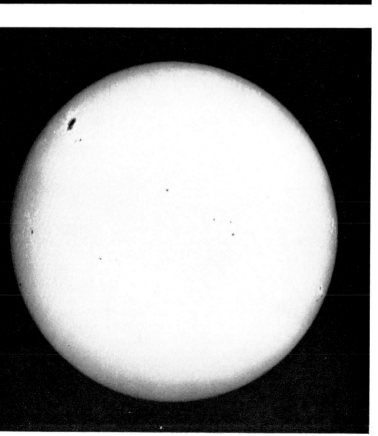

Both photos by A. Müller, Zürich

XIII. (*left*): The Sun photographed at the focus; reflector, 135 mm. diameter and 9500 mm. focal length. *Actual size.* (*right*): The Moon photographed at the focus, with the same instrument. Again *actual size.*

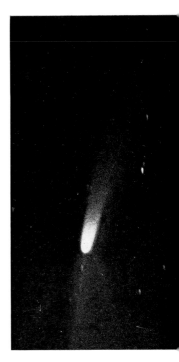

Peter Hückel, Weilheim

XIV. Section of the Moon photographed by means of the projection method. 17/10 DIN emulsion, exposure 2 seconds, 10″ reflector.

XV. Comet Arend-Roland 19 Photographed by an amateur, Kimberger, Fürth.

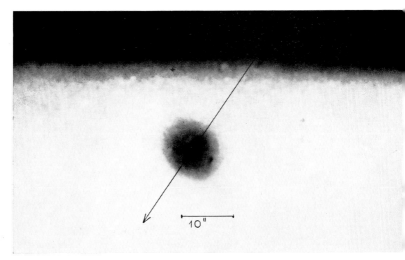

10″

XVI. Mercury on the face of the Sun 1960, November 7th. Photographed by an amateur, A. Müller, Zurich. Enlarged ×45 from a negative taken at the focus, with diameter of Sun about 95 mm. (compare with Plate XIII).

VIII

The Bright Rays on the Moon

Julius Franz, a lunar observer, once said that the Moon was a world inhabited only by minerals. Nevertheless our nearest neighbour in space is an interesting world. The observer sees through his telescope a rugged landscape, with mountains and valleys, and there is no lunar atmosphere to obscure the view. Selenography has been described as a region of relative calm amid the rushing torrent of advances in modern astrophysics. It is fairly true to say that Mädler's 'Mappa Selenographica' (published in 1838) is still considered fundamentally accurate, although, of course, additions have been made to it.

Since the death of Philipp Fauth in 1941, the nerve centre for lunar observation seems to have moved to Britain and the U.S.A. Here in recent years a great deal of painstaking work, chiefly by amateur observers, has advanced the study of the lunar surface, one might almost say, to the point of perfection. Closely associated with such advances must be the names of two British observers, the late H. P. Wilkins and Patrick Moore, both of whom have done a great deal to stimulate general interest in our natural satellite.*

* An excellent introduction to a study of the Moon is Patrick Moore's *Survey of the Moon*, published by Eyre & Spottiswoode.

The more advanced observer might prefer *The Moon*, by H. P. Wilkins and Patrick Moore, published by Faber & Faber, which is basically a description of Wilkins' map.

The Bright Rays on the Moon

Doubtless many an observer will find serious difficulty in producing neat and accurate drawings of his observations. Unfortunately, not all of us are gifted in the use of a pencil, and however hard we may try, our results will fall far short of the excellent work produced by some observers. I would therefore like to suggest a line of activity which does not place quite so high a demand on artistic ability, yet is full of interest, namely the study of bright rays on the lunar surface. Almost everyone will have seen these phenomena, either with the naked eye, or through a pair of binoculars, and wondered about their origin. It must be admitted that no definite answer has so far been found to this question; in fact the same applies to the whole problem of the origin of the Moon itself and the formation of the surface features. Many theories have been advanced, but none is entirely flawless. No doubt the Moon is a body which invites a great deal of comparison with geological facts.

The bright rays are most easily seen under high light. Nevertheless the rays emanating from the crater Tycho have also been observed at other times, even fairly close to the terminator. These rays from Tycho form the most prominent of the lunar ray systems. Of the other systems that of Copernicus is perhaps the most typical, the rays being shorter and filament-like, and giving an overall appearance which is similar to a spider's web. Those emanating from Tycho, however, are distinctive in that they are particularly bright and broad and stretch far across the visible lunar surface. Especially interesting is the way in which they sometimes stop short of craters lying in their paths and then continue once more beyond the obstacles. The rays also vary in the way in which they traverse regions of the Moon which at low Sun show themselves to be extremely undulating. The observer has to look out for numerous light patches or craterlets in chain formations—since these can be confused with the rays, or alternatively may influence the course of the latter.

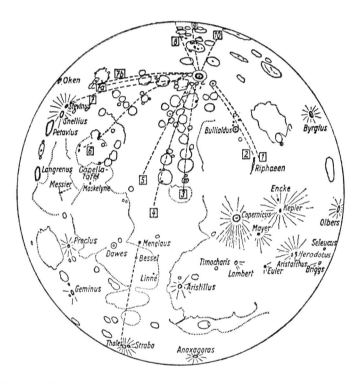

Fig. 12. Sketch map of Moon showing the principal bright rays (F. Billerbeck-Gentz). The paths of rays emanating from the crater Tycho are as follows:

RAY 1. *Start:* south of Heinsius. *Continuing through:* Cichus, Kies, König. *End:* Lubiniezky E to Riphæan Mountains.

RAY 2. (westerly companion of 1) *Start:* east of Sasserides A. *Continuing through:* Wurzelbauer, east of Hesiodus and Bullialdus B, Bullialdus, Lubiniezky. *End:* Riphæan.

The Bright Rays on the Moon

RAY 3. *Start:* west of Sasserides. *Continuing through:* Regiomontanus, Purbach, Thebit, Ptolemæus. *End:* north of Spörer (the continuation into Sinus Medii is doubtful).

RAY 4. *Start:* Lexell. *Continuing through:* west of Regiomontanus, Parrot, Alhategnius, Hipparchus. *End:* west of Sinus Medii.

RAY 5. *Start:* north of Orontius. *Continuing through:* Walter, Abulfeda, *End:* Descartes.

RAY 6. *Start:* south of Orontius. *Continuing through:* Stöfler, Gemma Frisius, Altai, Fracastor E. *End:* Mare Nectaris.

RAY 7. *Start:* south-west of Tycho near Saussure. *Continuing through:* Maurolycus. Splits into 7a and 7b. 7 ends near Stevinus, 7a near Metius, and 7b between Metius and Fabricius.

RAY 8. *Start:* Maginus. *Continuing through:* Clavius, west, Gruenberger. *End:* South Pole.

RAY 9. *Start:* Longomontanus, west. *Continuing through:* Clavius, east, Wilson. *End:* Dörfel.

RAY 10. *Start:* between Tycho and Longomontanus. *Continuing through:* Longomontanus, east wall of Scheiner, *End:* west of Bailly.

For this sort of work the amateur needs no more than a two- or three-inch telescope, and the magnification should be such that most of the lunar disc is visible in the field of vision, though naturally a higher power may be used from time to time for such detail studies as are necessary. In order to establish some kind of uniformity in the observation programme the problem should be tackled in the manner suggested by Friedrich Billerbeck-Gentz, an observer who did much useful work in the investigation of the rays. The observer should set out to answer the following questions:

1. Where does the ray begin?
2. How does it run?
3. Where does it end?
4. How broad is it?
5. How bright is it?
6. Does the brightness of the ray vary along its length

84

or in its breadth, and if so at what places and at what times?

7. What is the general nature of the surface within the ray? Could it be that the effect is simulated by a row of bright patches (isophotes), or perhaps bright craterlets, or even undulations in the surface?

8. The shape of the ray: for what distance does it run straight; where does it bend; where do the gaps occur, and how wide are such gaps?

9. Are there any features in the ray which have a distinctive colouring in certain lighting conditions when the rest of the ray is not visible?

10. When do the rays appear and when do they disappear?

It will be found in the course of one's study of these bright rays that one soon acquires quite a wide knowledge of the lunar surface as a whole. There are plenty of maps or photographs of the Moon available to-day, and these provide an excellent means of orientation. Moreover, large-scale photographs lend themselves as templates for drawing in the rays; all that one needs to do is to clip some tracing paper over the photograph and simply draw in the ray on this. The method has another asset: because some of the rays cover extensive distances, it is extremely difficult to draw in all the main features along their paths exactly in their correct positions.

Initially it is advisable not to try to be too ambitious, but to keep the observing programme fairly limited; for instance, to work on just one ray from the crater Tycho, but to do this really thoroughly. One must first learn to find one's way around on the Moon; the real danger in lunar observation is that the beginner can easily become

The Bright Rays on the Moon

lost among the multitude of features to be seen with even a fairly small instrument. This being so, it is as well never to be over-hasty in claiming to have discovered something 'new'. Moreover, the limb regions, in particular, are still not charted as accurately as is desirable, and in this field the method of direct observation is still of extreme value, despite the advance of lunar photography.

Serious lunar observation demands that the details should be studied under varying lighting conditions. For example, a particular feature should be examined when the Moon is waxing, while the Moon is full, and when it is waning. The shadows on the lunar surface undergo considerable changes with the varying angle of the Sun; so much so that some features can take on a completely different appearance under changed lighting conditions, a fact that has often proved a trap for the unwary. In any case, one can learn much from the changing shadows in a particular crater, even over a relatively short time, and it is fascinating to watch individual mountain peaks just inside the dark hemisphere come into view as the Sun rises on them and the terminator recedes, isolated gleaming points of light against the dark background.

IX

Observing the Occultations of Stars

It is hardly surprising that in the course of the year the Moon appears frequently to pass in front of some bright stars, obscuring them from the view of observers on Earth. The occasion is particularly interesting when the bright star lies in the path of the waxing Moon, subsequently to be obscured by the latter. The star then disappears behind the eastern limb of the Moon, and after a certain interval reappears from behind the western limb. In the period following on new moon, when it appears as a thin crescent, most of the disc will be unilluminated, but as result of 'earth-shine' which is due to sunlight reflected from the Earth, this portion of the face will not be entirely dark; instead it will be suffused with a faint glow of light. Hence the shape of the Moon will be seen quite distinctly against the much darker background of the sky. The bright star is seen to approach the dark limb of the Moon, and then very suddenly vanish from the observer's view; so much so, that the observer can easily be caught unaware and forget to note the exact time.

This brings us to the question of how one should go about making such observations. A reliable and accurate clock is the first essential for this purpose, and the reader should refer once more to p. 42. Unless one feels the urge to observe very faint stars, a small instrument, even field-glasses, will prove perfectly adequate. A two-, or three-inch telescope is certainly equal to all demands. No great magnification is needed, and for the instruments just mentioned I would suggest a power between ×20 and ×50.

The exact timing of the moment of occultation is of interest to astronomers, since it helps in calculating the position of the Moon, and this in turn is used in the study of the Earth's rotation. For these reasons careful amateur observations are always very welcome, and the international centre for such work is at the Royal Greenwich Observatory, now situated at Herstmonceux Castle in Sussex.

How can one discover when and where an occultation will take place? The relevant information is always to be found in astronomical yearbooks, and such publications as the *Handbook* of the British Astronomical Association. The latter lists all occultations of planets and of stars down to magnitude 7·5. It is important to remember that the actual times of occultation and reappearance depend largely on the location of the place from which the observation is made. If the observation is to be made from a place not too far from the station for which the times quoted in a particular table have been calculated, then the times of immersion and emersion may be worked out from a simple formula. The time of occultation at a place $\Delta\lambda$ degrees *west* and $\Delta\phi$ degrees *north* of the station for which the prediction is given may be found from: Predicted time $+ a.\Delta\lambda + b.\Delta\phi$, in which the co-efficients a and b are given in the table in terms of minutes. If the place of observation is *east* of the station, then $\Delta\lambda$ is taken as negative; similarly $\Delta\phi$ is negative if the observer is *south* of the station.

Observing the Occultations of Stars

For distances up to 300 miles the error will not usually exceed two minutes.

A better result is obtained by using values of a and b for a latitude midway between the observer and the nearer station. If ϕ_1, a_1, b_1 apply to this station, and ϕ_2, a_2, b_2 to the other then

$$a = a_1 + \frac{\Delta\phi}{2(\phi_2 - \phi_1)}(a_2 - a_1) \quad b = b_1 + \frac{\Delta\phi}{2(\phi_2 - \phi_1)}(b_2 - b_1)$$

Example: Obs. at Manchester: $\lambda = 2° \; 14' \; W$
$$\phi = 53° \; 29' \; N.$$

Occultation of 302 B. Tau on Jan. 30

$$a_1 = -1 \cdot 7 \quad b_1 = -0 \cdot 6 \quad \phi_1 = +51° \; 29'$$
$$a_2 = -1 \cdot 4 \quad b_2 = +0 \cdot 2 \quad \phi_2 = +55° \; 55'$$
$$\Delta\lambda + 2 \cdot 2 \quad \Delta\phi + 2 \cdot 0$$

whence

$$a = -1 \cdot 7 + 0 \cdot 23(+0 \cdot 3) = -1 \cdot 6$$
$$b = -0 \cdot 6 + 0 \cdot 23(+0 \cdot 8) = -0 \cdot 4$$

Approx. time at Manchester

$$= 19^h \; 48^m + 2 \cdot 2(-1 \cdot 6) + 2 \cdot 0(-0 \cdot 4)$$
$$= 19^h \; 48^m \cdot 8$$

These formulæ have been taken from the *Handbook* of the B.A.A., which is an extremely valuable publication for the amateur observer. Among other things it gives details of all occultations during the year for the following stations: Greenwich, Edinburgh, Cape, Johannesburg, Wellington (N.Z.), Dunedin (N.Z.), Melbourne and Sydney (Aust.).

One may wonder whether there is really any need to work out this difference in time, since it is only a matter of a minute or so at the most. The point is that the accuracy called for in the timing of occultations must be within one-tenth of a second, and the disappearance or the re-emergence of a star happens so suddenly that it demands the whole-hearted concentration of the observer, so that he must know the exact time.

The best way to get the timing right is to work with a stop-watch. Even so, the procedure is not quite so simple as it may appear at first glance, for there will always be a definite time lapse between the actual sighting of the occultation and the stopping of the watch. This difference will depend mainly on how quickly a particular observer can react; not only does the reaction time vary for individual observers—usually between 0·1 and 0·3 seconds— but it will also vary with the physical state of the observer at the time of making the observation. It is therefore advisable to make one or two tests to find out exactly how much to allow for. One way of doing this is to stick a piece of paper over the watch so that about three-quarters of the face is obscured. Having set the watch going, one then waits for the second hand to appear from behind the mask, pressing the knob to stop the watch as soon as one sees it. The amount by which the hand has emerged indicates the time one has taken to react, and also gives the mechanical reaction of the watch being used, since this is not instantaneous either. The best thing is to make three or four such tests either just before or just after observing an occultation, and then take the mean value.

The log for any occultation observation should contain the following data:

1. Name or number of occulted body as given in the catalogue.
2. Time of occultation and/or reappearance in GMT;

it is as well always to put in the abbreviation GMT or UT (Universal Time), since it is not really a great deal of extra work, and definitely prevents any subsequent confusion. Also the time should be given correct to one-tenth of a second, bearing in mind that even with the best intentions the errors are not likely to be less than ± 0·2 seconds.

3. The geographical definition (latitude and longitude) of the observing station. This information can be found on relevant Ordnance Survey maps which can always be consulted in the local public library. Calculation of latitude and longitude should be as accurate as possible, and a rough estimate is not sufficient.

4. A brief description of the instrument used in the observation, i.e. whether reflector or refractor, focal length, diameter, and the power of the eyepiece.

5. A brief account of the method of observation, indicating timing procedure, e.g. source of timing control—B.B.C. pips, etc.

Occultations of planets occur more rarely than those of stars, and information about these can always be found in astronomical handbooks. If one of the larger planets is being occulted there will be two contacts to record at occultation and two more on re-emergence. Because these bodies show discs, they do not disappear behind the Moon all at once. Therefore it is necessary to record the time when the leading edge of the planet 'touches' the limb of the Moon (first contact) and also when the trailing edge finally disappears behind it (second contact); the same thing happens when the planet re-emerges from behind the Moon.

Observing the Occultations of Stars

Occasionally we are allowed to witness some extremely rare events such as the occultations by the Moon of the satellites of another planet. This was the case in 1956, when two of Jupiter's moons were occulted, not once, but several times. However, such phenomena do not occur very often.

The planets can, of course, also occult stars, and, when a bright star disappears behind one of the planets (or one of the larger moons of Jupiter), apart from timing the phenomenon, observation of any changes in the brightness of the star is also an important factor. Not only can this give us data concerning the planet's atmosphere, but it can also tell us if the occultation is central or only partial.

All in all, there is much useful work to be done in this field.

X

Observing the Planets

The major planets have long been a favourite subject of study for amateur astronomers: Mars with its reddish tint and changing polar caps; Jupiter with its striped appearance and many moons; Saturn with its ring system, unique in the Solar System; all these are truly splendid sights in the telescope, and even a modest instrument—say, two inches in diameter—is able to reveal some of their magnificence.

However, anyone intending to study surface details on these bodies will need to avail himself of a more powerful instrument, something in the nature of four, six, or, if possible, eight inches in diameter. The most important aspect of planetary observation is the making of drawings of the features one can see on the surface—or, in some instances, the atmospheric mantles—of the planet under observation. In many respects this is easier than in the case of the Moon, for, even if one uses a large telescope and high magnification, the image of the planet always remains relatively small; thus the drawing is simpler, more in the nature of an outline sketch, without so many fine details and an absence of perspective. Nevertheless planetary observation is not just a matter of putting one's eye to a telescope and drawing a picture; much practice is required, but the work will be found both interesting and rewarding, as well as instructive.

Observing the Planets

In order that the matter of relative sizes may become absolutely clear, the following table will be found of interest. To obtain an image of the planet in the telescope the same size as the full moon *as seen with the naked eye* one should use:

PLANET	POWER	
Mercury	× 280	(elongation)
Venus	× 70	(elongation)
Mars	× 70	(opposition)
Jupiter	× 40	(opposition)
Saturn	× 100	(opposition)
Uranus	× 500	(opposition)
Neptune	× 750	(opposition)

By way of comparison, it is interesting to draw the face of the Moon as it appears to the naked eye. A subsequent comparison of this drawing with a chart of the Moon can prove extremely enlightening. W. H. Pickering, the well-known American astronomer, has drawn up a sort of observation test using twelve features to be seen on the Moon (Plate IX). He starts with Copernicus and its environs as being one of the easiest features to distinguish, and each successive object is slightly more difficult to see than its predecessor. With good average sight, one should be able to get to about number seven in the list. Numbers 10 and 11, let alone 12, call for very keen sight indeed.

The beginner may wonder whether his observations can ever reveal anything which professional astronomers with their vastly superior resources have not observed countless times already, or that photographic methods can produce more accurately and more readily. Such would indeed be the case were it not for the fact that the Earth's atmosphere constitutes an obstacle which becomes increasingly more difficult to overcome as the diameter of the telescope becomes greater. And, in any case, the giant telescopes which the professional uses are usually devoted to other aspects of astronomy. So far as photography is concerned, it is probably true to say that it has proved disappointing as a means of studying the planets; not that it has not fulfilled some useful functions, but in many respects direct visual observation has produced better results. So far the majority of the experiments in this field—and here amateurs have also played their part—have had a greater significance from the purely technical aspect, rather than helping to increase our knowledge of the planets. The human eye still holds pride of place in planetary observation, and there is little likelihood of the situation undergoing a marked change in the foreseeable future, unless of course something truly remarkable happens in the field of photochemistry.

If a planetary observation is to make a useful scientific contribution, it has nowadays to be of far higher quality than used to be the case. At the turn of the century the main focus of attention was on topography. However, we now know that Mercury and Venus do not offer a great deal of prospect in this respect, and, so far as Mars is concerned, a study of fine detail is called for, which means using a more powerful instrument, while purely graphic reproductions of Jupiter and Saturn are in themselves not satisfying enough, and Uranus, Neptune, Pluto and the great swarm of asteroids do not lend themselves for this type of observation at all.

But as soon as the drawings made at the telescope form an integral part of a wider programme of study, or the scope of simple observation is extended by the application of some special piece of apparatus, then a new and vigorous sense of purpose will be felt. One way of extending the scope of visual observation is to concentrate on a particular feature of the body being observed; thus one can try to establish a rotation period (Jupiter, Saturn); alternatively one can keep a look out for meteorological phenomena (Mars, Venus). On Jupiter, for instance, the observer should give his attention to a particular light or dark marking, and determine the position of this on the disc. For Mars there are the so-called Martian clouds, whose direction of drift and behaviour can be recorded.

Each observation of this sort should be made with the ultimate objective in view. It is useless to try to use sketches of the overall state, such as drawings of the cloud belts of Jupiter, to determine the exact positions of chosen features and then use the findings to calculate the rotation period. This does not mean that overall pictures of the state of the planet are useless. Far from it, for they show the appearance of that planet at a particular moment of time, as seen with a particular instrument by a particular observer. Accurate position-determining, on the other hand, does not so much require an abundance of detail as the careful reproduction of a few specially chosen features, and relating these by means of a system of co-ordinates.

Let us take Jupiter* as an example. Phenomena in its atmosphere within the two larger and better-known rotation systems provide sufficient material for positioning; these take the form of light or dark spots, streaks and

* B. M. Peek has written a comprehensive book dealing with this planet: *The Planet Jupiter*, Faber & Faber, London, 1958.

XVII. The U.S. balloon satellite Echo I, 1960, August 19th. Photograph taken by an amateur, R. Hanke, Dusseldorf, using a Leica, object-
ns Hekto 13·5 cm. ($f = 1 : 4·5$), on Agfa Isopan Record film, exposure
time approximately 10 minutes.

XVIII. The constellation Cygnus with Echo I (luminous trail). Astro
amera, aperture 71 mm., focal length 250 mm., exposure 30 minutes
n Perutz-Astro plate. (Taken by Dr. Hans Vehrenberg at his private
observatory at Falkau, Black Fo rest.)

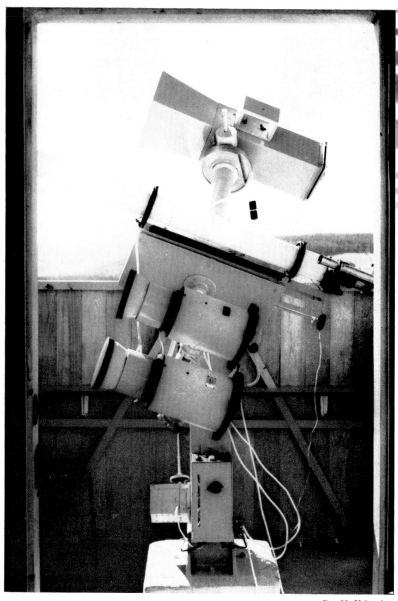

Dr. H. Vehrenberg

XIX. Refractor used as view-finder for three astro-cameras. Such cameras are relatively easy instruments for the clever handyman to make for himself.

indentations in the dark belts or light zones. The location of the bands in latitude does not change noticeably from one day to the next. Thus the observer can draw in the principal cloud belts and dark zones beforehand on a stencil outline. However, the latitudinal location of the belts does change over a period of weeks or months, so that it is unwise simply to take one's references from a drawing which might easily be out of date. Slight deviations from the actual Zenographic latitude may safely be ignored for this sort of work; what is important for determining the position of a particular feature is the longitude. Anyone who wishes to be really on the safe side, and has a fairly large telescope, can always measure the distance of the principal belts from the poles by means of a micrometer.

Having dealt with these preliminaries, the observation

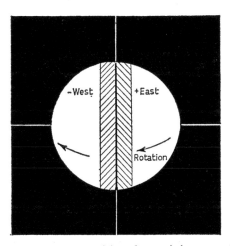

Fig. 13. Sketch for position-determining on Jupiter. The shaded area on either side of the central meridian indicates the region suitable for such observations. Nearer the limb, errors are more likely to creep in.

proper can begin, and one devotes one's attention to an area lying between 20 degrees east and 20 degrees west of the central meridian. The region of the disc nearer the limb is to be avoided, since there is more chance of observational errors creeping in. Let us assume that we have discovered a particularly prominent dark spot in the North Equatorial Belt, at about 10 degrees east of the central meridian. We next make a more precise calculation of its distance from this meridian, and mark its location on the stencilled outline, noting the time of observation accurate to about half a minute. After some five minutes we repeat the process, and so on, until the object has moved to roughly 10 degrees west of the meridian. Jupiter rotates so rapidly about its axis that an hour's observation will yield a number of determinations on either side of the central meridian.

The observation can then be evaluated by using a transparency marked off in the orthographic co-ordinates. In this way the individual positions recorded can be read off relative to the central meridian, east + and west − . The central meridian for each of the two main rotation systems will be given in any astronomical handbook, and so it takes no more than a simple calculation to work out the longitudinal position of the spot. Despite its apparent simplicity, this method is surprisingly accurate. After a little practice, the human eye soon becomes adept at judging the distances of certain features from the central meridian on small elliptical or circular discs. It is also possible to assess the actual moment at which a particular feature on the disc of a planet passes through the central meridian. Incidentally, it is better on the whole not to use stencil outlines of too large a scale, since this tends to lead to greater errors when the positions are plotted. For Jupiter the diameter of the outline should be something in the nature of $1\frac{1}{2}$–$2\frac{1}{2}$ inches.

Walter Löbering is a German observer who has had many years' experience and specialises in observing Jupiter. In his opinion a practised observer can well maintain an accuracy averaging between $\pm 0\cdot 5$ and $1\cdot 0$ degree. The beginner will, of course, not be quite so accurate to start with, but even so he should endeavour to attain a precision of $\pm 1\cdot 0$ degree, and eventually to improve on this. Larger features, such as the Great Red Spot on Jupiter, entail the plotting of the leading edge, the centre and the following edge.

This *modus operandi* for making observations of Jupiter also applies—with certain reservations—to Saturn and Mars. However, the apparent diameter of the disc of Jupiter is greater than that of either of the other two, and the atmosphere of the planet offers the amateur astronomer a great variety of features for carrying out his observations. While it is perfectly all right to make the stencils for Mars and Venus absolutely circular, both Jupiter and Saturn show appreciable polar compression, and therefore the outline should be elliptical rather than circular. The effect of phase and waxing and waning apparent diameter is most noticeable in the case of Venus. Mars is also subject to similar effects, though here the phases are not nearly so pronounced. On the whole, however, it is advisable to keep to a standard size for all drawings.

A planet such as Jupiter, which has a rapid axial rotation, offers the observer, provided that he has the endurance to observe the night through, the opportunity of seeing the planet make one whole revolution on its axis. The time to observe this is during the weeks preceding and succeeding opposition. In this way the whole of Jupiter's atmospheric mantle can be observed—an interesting though arduous task for the beginner.

Another way of going beyond the purely basic visual observation is to be found in the use of coloured filters. Such filters are not designed to reduce the light or to produce contrast. Instead they will let through only the light in a specific range of the spectrum. Filters for this purpose have to be very precise and of the highest quality; they must be ground smooth and tinted in the glass. For our purposes we shall need filters whose absorption-curve is fairly steep; those with a more gradual curve, letting through a little of several colours, are not really suitable.

Venus and Mars are subjects which lend themselves readily to visual observation with filters. I would advise first of all using Schott filters OG 5 (orange) and VG 6 (green). Then, having got the feel of things, one might go on to experiment with filters RG 2 (deep red) and BG 12 (blue).

The use of filters for making observations of the planet Venus has yielded varying results. But this planet is by no means an easy telescopic object, and the beginner should approach it warily. Most of the filter work to date has been done on Mars. So much so, that some firms producing optical equipment have on the market what they term 'Mars Filters' (orange–red). If such a filter is to be used, then it is necessary from the outset to find out what its absorption range is. The atmosphere on Mars is subject to great changes in transparency and cloud formation, so that its appearance varies not only with the type of filter, but also with the conditions prevailing on the planet at the time of observation. Thus one of the more rewarding tasks for the amateur observer is that of determining which filter gives the best results at any one time.

During the opposition of Mars in 1956, viewing conditions were often unusually poor, and surface details were obscured. Even the orange–red 'Mars Filters' proved of little avail. The cause for this was the extensive obscuration and opacity of the Martian atmosphere. I observed the planet during this period, using a deep-red filter (RG 2) with a seven-inch reflector, and I was surprised at the penetrative power, particularly as the view with an orange filter (OG 5) was so much poorer.

Normally a blue filter allows us the least view of the surface of Mars, but instead clouds high in the Martian atmosphere show up as brilliant white patches. Observation of the planet through a blue filter can prove extremely exciting, particularly as the degree of penetration can vary in a relatively short period of time, and as a result one has constantly to be on the alert.

Visual observation of the planets incorporating the use of colour filters offers the amateur plenty of opportunity for extending the scope of normal observation, and, as a result, allows us to learn yet more. However, the observer will be a little too optimistic if he expects the use of filters to yield him startling new revelations; though, in effect, the procedure will give his observations additional dimensions, in comparison with the flatness of ordinary visual observation. The Journals of the British Astronomical Association of 1961 and 1962 carry articles by a number of authors on the use of filters in planetary observations. There are some fairly conclusive results based on actual practical experience.

In closing, it should be mentioned that for a number

of reasons a reflecting telescope is better suited to this type of work than a refractor. For one thing, the chromatic correction of the object-lens of a refractor must obviously be outstandingly good, and a precise knowledge of the residual error is essential.

XI

Photographing the Sun, Moon and Planets

The amateur astronomer can gain a great deal of pleasure and experience by combining his observations with photography. The first thing which must be remembered is that when one is taking photographs of the Sun, the Moon or any of the larger planets, the optics of the telescope replace the camera lens. This is because all these subjects show discs, and the idea is to show as much of the disc as possible. For photographic work best results will only be obtained if the telescope has a fairly long focus. Refracting telescopes present some difficulty as a rule when it comes to photographic work. This is because the object-lens is usually corrected for direct visual observations. This means that the wavelengths of light to which the eye is most sensitive, i.e. yellow–green, are brought to the same focal point, but the rest, particularly the red on the one side and the blue on the other, then produce a slight, coloured rim, which is especially noticeable with bright objects such as the Moon, or Venus. For photographic work this effect is a nuisance, particularly the blue radiations. In ordinary landscape photography the difficulty of too much blue in the distance is obviated by using a yellow filter together with orthochromatic film or plate; the same method can also be used for astronomical photography. Since the degree of chromatic correction is by no means identical for each and every lens, it is best to try to determine the optimum photographic focus without filters by a method of trial and error. As a general rule, however, it is safe to say that photographs taken with filters tend to come out better, that is to say sharper, than those taken without. The owner of a reflecting telescope will not come up against such difficulties; his instrument is free from colour aberration, and is thus particularly suitable for photographic work.

The disc of the Sun appears virtually the same size as that of the Moon, and in the case of these two bodies we can take it as a very rough guide that for every metre of the focal distance the diameter of the image at the focus will be 10 millimetres. The situation is not quite so favourable when it comes to planets. Here the images formed in the focus can be reckoned only in fractions of millimetres, and thus, if one is to obtain a reasonable picture even of the giant Jupiter, the amateur would have to possess a telescope with a focal length of at least two to three metres ($6\frac{1}{2}$–10 feet).

There is a way of increasing the focal length of a telescope: the introduction of a negative achromatic lens, known as a *Barlow lens*. This will increase the focal length of the objective, or mirror, by the factor $\times n$. The value of n is given by the formula: $n = F_B/(F_B - A)$. Here F_B indicates the focal length of the Barlow lens, while A is the distance of the Barlow lens from the focal plane of the eyepiece. The use of such a system will add no more than a few centimetres to the structural length of the telescope. Not only will the increased focal length provided by the Barlow lens be useful for photographic work, but also for direct, visual observation.

Basically the amateur has two ways of setting about

his work. He can either capture the image formed at the focus, or alternatively he can use the image enlarged and projected by the eyepiece on to the photographic emulsion. This latter method has the advantage that the size of the image on the negative is fairly big to start with, so that the resolution of details on the positive print will almost certainly be better. On the other hand, the light intensity of this larger, projected image is not so great as that of the image formed at the focus. This does not matter when one's subject is the Sun, but for

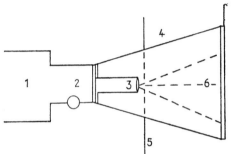

1. Telescope
2. Eyepiece sleeve
3. Eyepiece
4. Camera housing
5. Filter support
6. Photographic plate

Fig. 14. Diagram showing the projection method.

the Moon and the planets it plays an important rôle, since it entails a longer exposure time, which in turn demands an even and accurate following of the telescope; otherwise the resulting images could easily be blurred.

From the purely technical point of view it is easier to photograph at the focus, at any rate so far as the Sun and the Moon are concerned. Both these bodies may be photographed with a stationary instrument, as the exposure periods involved are usually no more than fractions of a second, and also, of course, the images of the Sun and the Moon produced on the negative will be sufficiently large—this latter is based on the assumption that the average focal distance of telescopes possessed by amateur observers is somewhere between one and two metres. A Sun or Moon negative of 10 or 20 mm diameter can easily be enlarged to 15 to 20 cm. For those who do their own enlarging I would suggest that they take a good sharp negative of the Sun or Moon about 20 mm across and try to blow it up to some 40–50 cm diameter, just to see what sort of picture can be obtained.

Both methods, photographing at the focus and projection, require that the instrument be set absolutely sharp prior to each exposure. For holding the plate or film, as well as a ground-glass screen for fine focus, we must either use a suitable camera body, or make our own Moon-and-Planet camera, such as the one which Hans Oberndorfer in Munich has been using with great success for years. Those who are lucky enough to possess a single lens reflex camera can simply use the body without the lens for this type of work. If, as in this instance, there is a built-in shutter mechanism, this can in fact prove very convenient. It should, however, be noted that some types of focal-plane shutters occasionally cause a slight vibration, which in this kind of work can easily blur the image. For this reason it is necessary to take every precaution not to jolt the instrument, be it ever so slightly, when the shutter is released to make the exposure. One way of getting round this difficulty is to use an auto-release—some cameras have these built in— together with a cable release.

The revolution of the Earth on its axis causes all celestial bodies to appear to move across the sky. This means that, having focused the instrument so that a particular body is centrally placed in the field of the

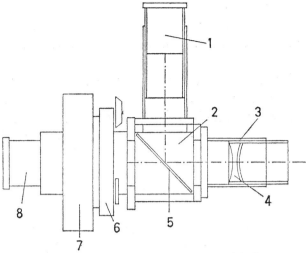

Fig. 15. Lunar and planetary camera with Compur
shutter and control eyepiece. (H. Oberndorfer.)

1. Eyepiece with hair cross
2. Wood or metal cube
3. Connecting Sleeve
4. Adjustable Barlow lens
5. Glass plate (inclined at 45°)
6. Shutter
7. Cassette
8. Magnifying focus

telescope, it will disappear from view after a few seconds
unless the telescope is moved so as to follow this motion.
Thus it can happen that what sets out to be a photograph
of the crescent Moon, in actual fact, shows no more than
just one tip of the crescent. There are two answers to
this problem: one can either swing the telescope to follow
the apparent motion of the subject, or one can set the
telescope to allow for the subject to drift across the field
of vision and expose when one thinks the subject is more
or less centrally placed. For the first of these methods
an important prerequisite is that the movement of the
telescope about its axis should be absolutely smooth and
regular, or results will be blurred. This is not all that easy
to achieve, and so the second method would seem to

offer the better prospect of success. One can soon become quite expert in judging how fast the subject appears to drift across the field, and then catch it at just the right moment.

The instrument needs to be focused accurately each time an exposure is to be made. This should be done by means of a ground-glass screen, with not too grainy a texture. The process is made all the easier if a magnifying lens is used to ensure that the image really is crisp when it is enlarged. There are no general rules for getting the right focus at the first attempt; it is always a matter of trial and error, and usually plenty of both. But after a little practice one soon begins to get the feel of things, and as one becomes more experienced, so the quality of one's pictures will also improve.

The dimensions of the negatives should be 24 × 36 mm for film, or 6 × 9 cm for plates. The normal type of roll-film with a paper backing, such as 120, 620, or 127, is not really suitable for our purposes, since the film plane is not sufficiently even. There is, of course, nothing against using plates of larger dimensions, except that it is more expensive. So far as the actual emulsion (film speed) is concerned, something like 17/10 DIN (= 50 ASA) panchromatic cut films or plates are probably the best types for the beginner. For solar work there is no reason why one should not use 12/10 DIN, or even less sensitive emulsions. Cut film and plates of 17/10 DIN are readily available, and, used in conjunction with fine-grain developers, are the least troublesome; moreover, they also have the advantage that they are fairly tolerant as regards the exposure time.

Anyone anxious to use the shortest possible exposure times can experiment using 23/10 or 25/10 DIN pan emulsions (approximately 200 ASA). For lunar work the coarser grain of this material will not detract from the quality of the final results, but for planetary work such an effect is to be avoided. There are also one or two thin emulsion films with fine grain and high contrast (12/10 to 15/10 DIN) and these are worth a trial. Using special developers, such as Neofin, sensitivity can be raised some 3–4/10 DIN. However, a great deal can be learned from experimenting with various types of emulsions and developers for individual subjects, and the foregoing is really only in the nature of a rough guide intended to spur on the reader. He will soon find out which combination suits his interests best.

The important points concerning the two methods of astronomical photography (focal and projection)* are tabulated on page 110.

* From the series 'Sterne, Fernrohre und Fotografen', by G. D. Roth, in Foto-Magazin, Dec. 1961 to March 1962.

FOCAL METHOD

	Sun	Moon	Planets
Negative size	fair	fair	small
Focal distance	from 1 metre	from 1 metre	from 3 metres
Definition of image	v. good	v. good	fair
Exposure time (seconds)	1/1000	1/5	1/5 to 1
Emulsion (DIN)	5–13	13–17	13–15
Enlargements		10–20 times the neg. diam.	
Effect of atmospheric turbulence	small	noticeable	considerable

PROJECTION METHOD

	Sun	Moon	Planets
Negative size	v. good	v. good	fair
Focal Distance	from 0·5 metre + eyepiece		from 2 metres + eyepiece
Definition of image	good	good	poor
Exposure time (seconds)	1/100	1 to 3	5 to 10
Emulsion (DIN)	5–13	17–21	13–15
Enlargements		2–5 times the neg. diam. of contact prints	
Effect of atmospheric turbulence	noticeable	considerable	very marked

For exposure times of 1 second or longer some form of slow-motion drive (either mechanical or manual) should be used to keep the image centred in the field.

This table should not be regarded as anything more than just a rough guide, and much depends on the type of telescope, the emulsion, and the time and place of observation. A useful meter for determining the exposure time is 'Lunasix'.

XII

Photometry

As the name implies, 'photometry' is concerned with measuring the intensity of the light which reaches us from celestial bodies, and forms an important branch of astronomical investigation. It is especially important in the study of those bodies on which we are unable to detect any surface detail. Here we must perforce rely for our information solely on the light which reaches us. Thus photometry plays a major rôle in stellar astronomy. But there are also bodies in our own Solar System, as for instance that multitude of little planets, the asteroids, which lend themselves for photometric observation.*

The light intensity of individual stars can be constant, or it can vary regularly or spasmodically. Then again these variations may be absolute or relative in respect of observation in different ranges of the spectrum. The human eye is particularly sensitive to light in the yellow–green range of the spectrum, while sensitivity for red or blue radiations is not nearly so good. Photographic emulsions, on the other hand, can be prepared so that they are sensitive to any given spectral range. This means that a star shining with yellowish light will seem

---

* A full account of these tiny bodies is contained in *The System of Minor Planets*, by G. D. Roth, published by Faber & Faber (1962).

brighter to the human eye than it will appear on a blue-sensitised photographic plate. These two differing impressions of the brightness of a particular celestial body in no way indicate that its light is variable; instead it does give us a factor which is known as the colour index. If we express the fact in terms of apparent magnitudes, we obtain the following result: visually the body has an apparent magnitude of, say, $4\cdot5^m$, while on a blue-sensitive plate the value appears as $5\cdot5^m$; the difference in the two values, $+1$, then gives us the amplitude for the colour index.

There are, however, bodies in the universe where a genuine variability in the intensity of their radiations over specific periods of time, be it their own luminosity (variable stars) or merely reflected sunlight (planets), has been shown, or is thought, to exist. The phenomenon is expressed as a light-curve, and is extremely important in astrometry. The total number of known variable stars and asteroids has meanwhile grown to such an extent that the number of observers in this field has not kept pace.

The basic task lies in measuring the intensity of the light which comes to us from suspect bodies, and then to see to what extent the intensity varies over a given period. Such observations can, of course, be carried out in various spectral regions, and the colour index, mentioned earlier, is then used as a guiding factor for comparison. In its simplest form stellar photometry consists of estimating the apparent brightness of a particular body, and fitting this into a suitable scale. The method has become universally known as the 'Argelander Step Method for Variable Stars'.

The equipment needed for making such estimates is

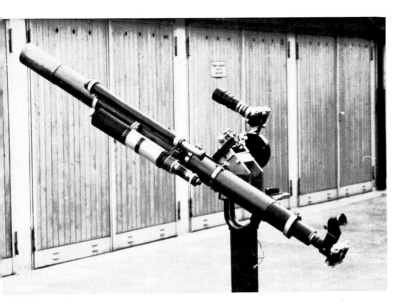

XX. Telescope constructed by J. Gewecke, Nuremberg. (*above*): The main tube has an achromatic objective of 86 mm. (3·4 inches); focal length 1500 mm. (59 inches); constructed from government surplus stock. There are two finders; camera fitted at the focus and a miniature camera as 'astrocamera'.

(*below*): More details: two prism-shaped aluminium alloy castings salvaged from a factory scrap heap form the nucleus of an extremely compact equatorial; a Siemens SH 41 220 volt synchromotor (6 watt consumption, 3000 r.p.m. geared 1 : 1200) provides the drive.

XXI. View of a 6" reflector of the Maksutov type, constructed by E. Popp of Zurich, an optician. Note the short structural length; although the focal length is

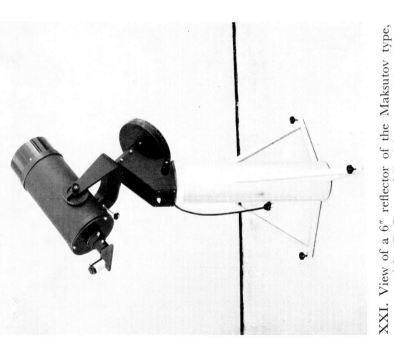

XXII. Front view of the binocular double telescope constructed by Heinz von Seggern. One can see the main mirrors and the 'flats'. The movable eye-piece

remarkably simple. Given some experience one can even carry out the work with the unaided eye, and binoculars are fully sufficient for the purpose, indeed they lend themselves extremely well. The wide field of vision is important here, since for the purpose of comparison a sufficient number of other stars must be observed simultaneously. On telescopes, low-power eyepieces should always be used, in order to make the observation more reliable; it is not only a nuisance to have to reset the telescope for the comparison stars, merely because these lie outside the field of vision, but also because in the process concentration is necessarily distracted from the real job in hand, so that errors are more likely to creep in.

The Argelander method works on the principle that the observed brightness of a body suspected to be variable is estimated relative to other celestial objects whose apparent magnitudes are not only constant, but also well known through many years of careful observation. The observed apparent magnitude of the suspect can then be integrated in a scale of stars of known magnitudes appearing in the same field. The choice as to what stars are to be used for making the comparison depends on the range of brightness to be bridged, as well as on the period. The more confined the whole star-field (variable + catalogue stars), and the finer the gradation of the scale, the greater becomes the accuracy of this method. A point worth watching is that observations should be confined to regions of the celestial sphere fairly close to the zenith, that is to say, not too low down in the sky near the horizon. Twilight, moonlight and any sort of artificial light sources will also detract from the quality of the observations made.

Photometry

The grading is done in the following way. First of all, stars to be used for making the comparison are arranged in order of apparent magnitude, and designated with letters of the alphabet, *a, b, c* and so forth. The variable star's magnitude can then be shown relative to two successive comparison stars, thus:

1. If the observer is unable to detect any difference in brightness between the variable (*v*) and the two comparison stars (*a* and *b*) even after careful scrutiny, he enters in his observation log: *aov, bov*.
2. If *a* appears slighly brighter than *v*, he writes: *a1v* (the brighter of two bodies is always placed first).
3. If the difference in brilliance is more considerable the observer can indicate the fact by writing: *a2v*.
4. If the difference in brightness is so obvious that it strikes one immediately, then one puts: *a3v*.

While such a classification of the magnitude can, of course, be extended *ad lib.*, either by adding to the range of whole numbers, or using fractions of the existing numerical scale, it must be realised that, far from increasing the precision, this usually tends to have the opposite effect. If the gap between the two catalogue stars used for comparison is indeed such as to make an extension of the range inevitable, then the situation is best remedied by closing the gap by choosing more suitable comparisons. From personal experience, I would say that the difference in apparent magnitude between any two successive catalogued stars should not be greater than $0\cdot5^m$.

A simplified example of the results of observations, in tabulated form, should look something like this:

DAY			TIME (GMT)	ESTIMATE	STEPS $a-b$	STEP VALUE for v
1962	Sept.	1	23h 10	a 1 v 2 b	3	1·25
,,	,,	2	22h 50	a 2 v 1 b	3	2·25
,,	,,	3	22h 40	a 3 v 1 b	4	2·75
,,	,,	4	23h 00	a 2 v 2 b	4	1·75
,,	,,	5	23h 10	a 1 v 3 b	4	0·75
,,	,,	6	23h 30	a 0 v 3 b	3	0·50

The sum of the numbers in column four is 21, and thence the mean value is 3·5. This mean value for the number of steps between one comparison star and the next will be required for making the ultimate evaluation. In the first observation (Sept. 1) star a is one step brighter than v, while b is two steps fainter than v. Now, if we take a, the brighter of the two comparison stars in our system, as being step 0·00, and b—calculated from the above-mentioned mean value—as step 3·5, then, in terms of the scale as a whole, the value of v relative to b is 1·5 (= 3·5 minus 2) steps brighter than b. This gives us two values $a:v$ and $v:b$, 1 and 1·5 respectively, and if we now work out the mean value of these two results we obtain the figure shown in column five, which is 1·25 in this particular example.

At first sight the whole thing may seem a little complicated and confusing, but it is really quite elementary statistics, and working on the basis of several means acts as a sort of safety device, which tends to ensure overall accuracy. The above example has in fact been considerably simplified, and in practice the series not only becomes longer, but several different comparison stars are used. However, the principle is the same. The values in column five express what has been observed, and may readily be used to show the maximum and the minimum brightness of the variable. If desired, the relative values from the scale may be converted to absolute values, i.e.

from comparative steps to magnitudes. For this we must know the magnitudes of the comparison stars, which we have already looked up earlier in the catalogue. The actual conversion is best performed by means of a graph. On the perpendicular axis (y-axis) we mark off the range of magnitudes of all the comparison stars, and on the x-axis (horizontal) the range of steps from the brightest to the faintest of the comparison stars. The appropriate step values are then plotted against their corresponding magnitudes. Finally we draw a straight line through the series of points we have marked; this is to even out any minor deviations. From this graph the magnitude corresponding to any particular step of the scale can then be read off without difficulty.

Most things are difficult, or appear so, to start with, and estimating the brightness of a celestial object is no exception. Stars which have a short-period variability should be left well alone by the beginner, and the same goes for any object fainter than about 10ᵐ. The observation of variable stars is not necessarily concerned with maxima *and* minima, for the recording of a maximum alone can be of interest. So far as the asteroids and long-period variables are concerned, the amateur observer must needs confine his activities to observations of only the maximum brightness.

The choice of suitable celestial subjects and finding them amongst all the other stars in the heavens is yet another hurdle which must be surmounted. It is possible to obtain charts of specific regions of the sky,* and there

* A working group of international standing is *The American Association of Variable Star Observers*, one of whose main functions is to give help to amateur observers in this field. The address is: Harvard College Observatory, Cambridge 38, Mass., U.S.A.

are also various handbooks in which lists and charts of suitable variables are given. But this still leaves the would-be observer the task of finding the star which he is after, or an asteroid of only about 8^m, as well as the comparison stars, among the myriads of stars visible in the sky. Fortunately there are usually one or two really bright stars in the neighbourhood of the star being searched for, and these can be used as guides, but first the beginner should make himself thoroughly familiar with the name and appearance of each of the principal constellations, for this is the initial step towards finding one's way around the firmament. In this way, with the help of a star map, one can move from star to star until one has found one's objective. When one has done this once and noted the position of the body in respect of a relevant constellation, it soon becomes quite easy to find the body again whenever one wants it.

In passing, it must be mentioned that this is not the only method for making photometric observations. One can, for instance, use a special instrument called a photometer.* Some of these use comparative light sources; others a system of graduated filters. Whichever type one decides to go in for, it will of course entail additional expenditure as well as being yet another piece of equipment to be looked after, whereas the beauty of the Argelander method lies in its simplicity. This is why so many observers use it. Furthermore, its precision can be increased to some extent if the eyepiece is set slightly out of focus, so that the stellar image, instead of being a

---

* Those interested in photo-electric photometry will find further information in *The Manual for Photoelectric Photometry*, obtainable from AAVSO, 4 Brattle Street, Cambridge 38, Mass., U.S.A., price $1.

point of light, distends into a disc; it is much easier for the eye to detect very small differences in intensity in this way, and an observer should be able to judge differences of as little as 0.1^m.

XIII

Shooting Stars

One of the very few branches of astronomy which can be undertaken without the use of any kind of optical instrument is the observation of meteors. One peculiarity of this province is that appearances of meteors can be predicted only roughly, at best within a matter of weeks or days. Even then there are numerous exceptions. One of the recurring variety, which can be predicted because they make their appearances at about the same time each year, are the Perseids, and most of us will have seen shooting stars belonging to this swarm during August. Though the visible life of a shooting star may be brief, it will nevertheless reveal several facts to the interested observer.

The majority of meteors range from small to very small, and, on entry into the Earth's atmosphere, all but a very small percentage of them vaporise completely as a result of the frictional heat generated. Meteoroids are cosmic bodies which, like the planets and comets, travel in definite orbits. From time to time the Earth will wander into the orbit of a swarm of meteors. Sometimes some of the larger meteors manage to penetrate the Earth's atmosphere until they come fairly close to the Earth's surface, and these are the cause of what we call fire-balls. Sometimes even the original body is so large that not all of it burns up in its passage through the atmosphere, and pieces of it actually strike our Earth. Fortunately this does not happen with great frequency, but the meteoric mass which fell in Tunguska in Northern Siberia early this century is an obvious and much-quoted example. At the other end of the scale there are also some meteoric particles which are so small that they cannot generate sufficient frictional heat in their passage through the air, and these minute micrometeorites also manage to reach the Earth's surface but without leaving a luminous trail.

Although the appearances of sizable meteors are but rare occurrences, there is every chance that such a phenomenon will be observed by a fairly large number of people interested enough to record the fact; and furthermore, if it is bright enough, it is likely that a number of observers in different parts of the Earth will see it, which will enable its path to be calculated. The important task at each sighting of a bright meteor (apparent magnitude about the same as that of the planet Jupiter) is to note the time and apparent path across the sky. So far as is possible the path of a fire-ball should be defined by means of the points of its appearance and disappearance. However, the point at which the fire-ball appeared will probably elude the observer because he would not be expecting its arrival; so the next best thing is for the observer to record the point at which he first saw the object. Apart from noting the point in the sky where the trail petered out, the observer lucky enough to make such a sighting should estimate the place on the horizon for which the object appeared to be heading. Finally one should also record the duration (a matter of seconds), what it looked like, its colour, any changes observed and any accompanying sounds. The apparent magnitude of the object can be adequately described in terms of the Moon, or the planets Jupiter or Venus.

Shooting Stars

If a fire-ball is seen at night, it is no difficult matter to describe its observed apparent path relative to the stars and constellations. So soon as he has made such an observation, the careful observer will immediately make a sketch of what he has seen and note the important data. If such a sighting is made during the day or in twilight conditions, one has to determine the apparent path with the help of geographic features. Here the important detail is the azimuth while, so far as the celestial direction is concerned, it should be remembered that we count from south (0 degrees) over west (90 degrees), north (180 degrees), east (270 degrees) and back to south again. The altitude above the horizon can be calculated roughly.

With regard to the observation of small meteor trails such as occur throughout the year with a lesser or greater degree of frequency, according to the time of year, the important factor is the number of sightings made within a specified period of time, usually one hour. For this the observer should confine himself to watching a particular region of one quadrant of the celestial hemisphere, preferably the east. For the duration of a particular series of observations (at least over one year) the region of one's choice should be rigidly adhered to. The count should be made only within the specified period of time (one hour), each night when the seeing is sufficiently good. For those amateur observers who are able to prise themselves from their beds, early morning observation is to be especially recommended.

Each observation should be accompanied by approximate data as to apparent brightness (relative to stars in the vicinity), data as to observing conditions (moonlight, haze, etc.) and last, though by no means least, the time and location of the observing station. In the course of such a series of systematic observations even the hours for which a nil return is made are significant; the fact that no meteors were seen should most certainly be noted in the observation log. The purpose behind this kind of meteor census is to discover a relationship between the frequency of meteors and the direction of the Earth's motion.

A further task is the observation of meteor trails in the night sky, and then plotting these on a star map. Once a sufficient number of such observations has been made, the centre from which these trails originate can be determined. This provides us with information on meteor streams. In order to determine the radiant from which the meteors seem to come, one needs at least three to four dozen observations. There is here no need to keep to a given time limit, as is the case in the purely statistical meteor count, but it is nevertheless advisable to gather the necessary data over a period of about one week to a fortnight.

The recording of meteor trails photographically is largely a matter of chance. The optical requirements for this kind of work are extremely high, and are likely to lie well beyond the reach of most amateur observers. However, if it should happen that in the course of making an exposure of a star field a meteor trail should be found on a photograph, this must not be regarded as no more than nuisance value. Instead it should be treated as an observation in its own right, and the relevant details logged, particularly the time when the exposure was made. Such chance successes can be used for determining the path of the body—provided that visual observations from other localities are also available—and may also be used for photometric evaluation. How one can 'twist the arm of fate' a little and improve one's chances of taking such photographs is explained in the chapter which follows. Experience has shown that improvements in the light-sensitivity of photographic emulsions not only make it possible to take photographs of meteors, but also make it a feasible proposition with a relatively small camera. For instance, anyone possessing a miniature camera fitted with a Zeiss Biotar 1 : 1·5/75 mm lens, and using the latest Agfa Record film (at least 34 DIN), stands an excellent chance of obtaining successful meteor photos.

Even with such standard optics as 1: 2·8, or 1: 3·5 (the kind fitted to a great many miniature cameras) and used in conjunction with a highly sensitive film emulsion, it is possible to photograph the trails of fairly bright shooting stars. Some excellent results have been obtained on Ilford HP5 film. The following experiment is well worth trying: train the camera on a region of the sky known to be rich in shooting stars (for this consult *Meteor Diary* in the *Handbook* of the British Astronomical Association); clamp the camera tight; and then expose for about 15 minutes.

XIV

Miniature Astrographs

The human eye is fallible, and one of the most dangerous faults, so far as astronomical observations are concerned, can be a preconceived idea in the mind of the observer. Subjective observation cannot always be ruled out, though fortunately photography can usually provide irrefutable evidence of the true facts. Here and there it can also be invaluable to the amateur observer.

Let us begin by considering the photographic images of point-like light sources—i.e. stars—such as are produced with ordinary cameras, various types of which are to be found on the market nowadays. For certain types of work the astronomical telescope plays the part of the camera lens. Here the dimensions of the field of view are very small, and so for stellar photography specially corrected and designed astro-cameras (astrographs) have to be used. Such valuable instruments—the ultimate of which is the well known Schmidt camera—are almost invariably outside the province of amateur astronomy. Precision work of this kind is extremely expensive. But the amateur can nevertheless equip himself with an astrograph of sorts at much less cost. Not only will this give him a camera which will serve him for astronomical purposes, but also one which will do for everyday work.

There is hardly a household to-day which does not boast at least one camera. Not all of these are suitable for astronomy. Older types of plate cameras with aperture ratios of 1:6 will, however, do perfectly well for the first attempts at astro-photography. The aperture ratio in itself is not the deciding factor as to whether the camera can be used for this type of work or not. It is the light-gathering power, i.e. the effective aperture, which is of importance in this respect. The camera lens must have an aperture of something like 20 to 30 mm, with not too great a focal length, if it is to be at all suitable. Modern roll-film and miniature cameras will, by and large, have the required qualifications.

Extremely powerful lenses fitted to some types of cameras ($f = 1:1.5$ or $1:2$) are not necessarily the best for our purpose. Even during a brief exposure, lenses of this kind can and do reproduce far too much stray light, as a result of which the whole picture is too light and the images do not stand out enough. Moreover the correction of some of these lenses, which have after all been designed for very different purposes, is not always the best for stellar photography; distortion towards the edge of the field is also a possibility. Most suitable are those types of lenses which are noted for the sharp, crisp images they produce, lenses made up of four elements. Whether the camera has a standard (fixed) or an interchangeable lens —apart from a few specialised instances—the focal length of the lens is usually between 75 and 200 mm, while the aperture lies between 20 and 50 mm; such values are quite adequate for a miniature astrograph. Most amateur photographers will probably recognise some of the names of some of these lenses: Elmar, Cassar, Tessar, Xenar, Primotar, Color-Skopar, Travenar and so forth.

The use of a telephoto lens is an advantage—especially in the case of a miniature camera—since the small scale produced by the normal lens of 50 mm or so focal length is not really suitable. Roughly the format should be such that the diagonal is equivalent to the focal length of the lens. For the photographing of star fields the ideal negative sizes are usually 6 × 6, 6 × 9 or 9 × 12. Anything larger (13 × 18) is, of course, still better, but sizes of this sort are likely to stretch the resources of the amateur a little too far.

When trying to make up one's mind what type of film to use for stellar photography, the choice should always be made in favour of sensitivity rather than graininess. Emulsions with speeds of 18/10 to 25/10 DIN lend themselves well. I have seen photographs taken on 25/10 DIN film, which have subsequently been enlarged to 20 × 30 cm, without the grain adversely affecting the quality of the star images. This is fairly conclusive proof that we do not have to take the coarseness of the grain into consideration quite so much as when we are making exposures of the Sun, Moon or planets. A higher film speed is achieved principally at the expense of the graininess of the emulsion, and, so far as the latter in no way spoils the result we are after, the higher speeds obviously offer an advantage; the exposure time does not have to be so long and there is therefore less chance of blurring. Film speed is an important factor when trying to take photographs of meteor trails and artificial satellites. With their Royal-X Pan film, Kodak Ltd. provide an emulsion with a sensitivity of 32 DIN, while the rating of Agfa's Isopan Record goes as high as 34 DIN! The more pronounced grain matters little, and either of these two types of film enables us to obtain first-class photographs of brightish shooting stars and earth satellites, such as the balloon satellite Echo I. Details of the latter's passage across our skies can be found in some daily newspapers, as for example the *Daily Telegraph*.

These highly sensitive emulsions make it possible to take photographs of star fields with an exposure time of only a few seconds. All stars visible to the naked eye will come out. Apart from using these and other common types of film the advanced amateur will probably at some time or other wish to use plates especially designed for astronomical work. One which has rendered good service is Kodak Tri-X type B, a new kind of panchromatic emulsion. One might describe it as a universal emulsion for amateur astromomers. For short exposures (up to about 10 minutes' duration) Kodak 103a-O and Kodak 103a-E have excellent characteristics. The last-named emulsion is especially effective in the red region of the spectrum, and is thus seldom used without a red filter.

On the packing of many plates and films it is suggested that they be stored in 'a cool place'. Cooled emulsions do indeed have a greater degree of sensitivity than those which are not cooled. Experiments at the U.S. Naval Observatory have shown that the exposure times required for cooled films or plates can be reduced to one-third of those for un-cooled emulsions.

Colour film is, of course, another thing altogether, but even in this field there is room for the amateur astro-photographer. I have myself experimented with my miniature camera using Kodachrome II reversal film and exposure times of 15 and 30 minutes. The impression of the various colours of the stars is unmistakable when one looks at the slide. The blue tint of the Pleiades agrees reasonably well with their spectral type—they are of the B type. On the other hand the Pole Star, which is of the F type, shows as yellowish-white. Stars of magnitude 6–7 will come out on Kodachrome II with an exposure time of some 25 minutes.

The question of ensuring adequate following with the camera is one which needs particular attention. The usual exposure time required is somewhere in the nature of half an hour. Longer periods demand especially favourable conditions: a location well away from any large urban area or other light sources which might cause interference. A half-hour or so exposure can easily be managed by means of manual guidance with a slow-motion drive, if a good equatorial mount is employed. All that is required is to attach the camera to the tele-scope tube; just how this can best be accomplished depends largely on the telescope and the ingenuity of the observer. Then the telescope is adjusted so that, using a fairly high power and an extra-focal setting, one of the brighter bodies in the star field to be photographed is kept constantly centrally placed (hair-line cross). If a form of mechanical drive is fitted, this should at first be regarded with the utmost suspicion; only after it has been extensively tested and found to be absolutely reliable —which is not often the case—should one entrust it with the task of guiding the camera during an exposure time of as long as half an hour. Should there be any doubt at all as to the precision of the motor drive, it is definitely better to stick to manual guidance, which can with practice be brought to a fine art.

What sort of results can the amateur expect from his albeit modest equipment?

A good four-element lens with an aperture of 30 mm ($f = 4\cdot5$) will without effort bring out stars down to magnitude 10 on a really dark night with an exposure time of 30 minutes. Development and enlarging of the

XXIII. Equatorial sundial in the grounds of the new Nautical School, Bremen. The school buildings can be seen in the background with the dome of the Olbers Observatory.

negative play an important part in determining the quality of the final result. The development of the film or plate can be carried out in the normal manner. If the observer cannot process them himself, it is not advisable to send them to the nearest chemist for this purpose without some words of explanation, for not all dark-room assistants are likely to have an eye for stars of *this* type! Processing one's own films undoubtedly gives greater pleasure and satisfaction. The enthusiast may be interested in trying 'Neofin blue' developer, which has proved most efficient for this sort of work; at 23° Centigrade (73·5° Fahrenheit) development takes about 25 minutes. Care should be taken at all times to avoid dirty solutions, dust and scratch marks. Experience has shown that it definitely pays to do one's own development and enlarging if it is at all practicable, particularly in the case of astronomical work. Where it is not possible to keep a special dark-room, cupboards, kitchens or bathrooms can always be commandeered, temporarily but effectively.

Rare phenomena, such as the appearances of bright comets, most recently the comet Seki-Lines (spring 1962), are subjects well worth attempting to photograph. The results obtained with the comet Arend-Roland, 1957, were indeed better than had been expected, and photographs of this sort are often the prize possessions of many an amateur astronomer.

Furthermore, it is possible, using only an ordinary camera to compile one's own star atlas. If stars of magnitude 8 or 10 are considered to be insufficiently inclusive, one can build oneself a camera especially for astronomical work; alternatively one could even buy one, though such instruments are by no means cheap. Special lenses, for example the kind used for aerial photography, can be obtained second-hand at very reasonable prices. A two- or three-inch astro-camera, with an aperture ratio of something between 1:3·5 and 1:5, can produce most remarkable results. An instrument of this sort should furnish the amateur with photographs of star fields which will include stars of magnitude 11 or 12. During 1960 and 1961 a German amateur astronomer, Dr. Hans Vehrenberg of Düsseldorf, completed a photographic star chart of the northern sky. His instrument consisted of a Zeiss Tessar lens with an aperture of 71 mm and a focal length of 250 mm. He uses mainly Kodak Tri-X (Type B) plates measuring 9 × 12; the normal exposure given was 30 minutes. An example of his work can be seen in Plate XVIII.

The best way to find out what can and what cannot be achieved is to experiment for oneself; all that I have tried to demonstrate is what can and has been done by amateurs. The opportunity is always there.

XV

Building a Sundial

Though sundials and telescopes are only distantly related, it seems that amateur astronomers will nevertheless be interested in them. A sundial is more than a mere ornament; it is the oldest time-telling instrument, and is a constant reminder of the regularity of the movements of the celestial bodies.

In its simplest form, a sundial shows what is termed 'apparent time'—due, of course, to the Earth's axial rotation together with its motion round the Sun. However, this differs from 'mean solar time', and the difference between the two is known as the *Equation of Time*. Since a sundial shows apparent solar time, the mean solar time may be obtained by applying the necessary correction.

Let us begin at the beginning. The Sun's maximum altitude above the horizon for each day varies according to the season, but it was realized, thousands of years ago, that some means of time-checking could be arranged by placing a stake in the ground, drawing a circle round it, and dividing the circle into equal parts. The length of the Sun's shadow had, of course, to be taken into account, and the method was very rough and ready, but it was better than nothing. Moreover, it led to the discovery that the time taken by the shadow to move from one division of the circle to the next was not constant, but varied according to the time of year.

Next, the ancient Egyptians and Babylonians found that if the stake were put in at an angle, instead of vertically, the trouble did not occur. In fact, if the stake is so placed as to lie parallel to the Earth's axis, the time taken by the shadow to move from one mark to the next remains constant throughout the year; the Sun's altitude above the horizon makes no difference. The accuracy of a sundial depends upon the correct positioning of the indicator relative to the Earth's axis, and to the positioning of the dial relative to the plane of the horizon. These two factors also determine the calibration of the dial. There are, therefore, various types of sundials, depending on whether the plane of the dial extends to the horizon or to the zenith, or to one of the geographical poles, or to the equator.

It need hardly be said that, when a sundial is set up, it must be sited so as to catch the Sun's rays for as long as possible; there is little point in erecting a sundial under a tree, for instance! With the vertical type of sundial, often found mounted on the south side of a building, the shadow of the indicator is thrown across the face of the dial so long as the Sun travels across the sky from east, through south to west. The indicator must, then, point south. In the southern hemisphere the Sun appears to move from the east, through north to west; the indicator must therefore point north. Obviously, this type of sundial is not very effective in the tropics, where the Sun passes sometimes south and sometimes north of the zenith.

The horizontal type of sundial will show the time, when and if the Sun shines, from sunrise to sunset; it can be viewed from any direction, and ornamental sundials of this kind can frequently be seen in public parks and in private parks (the same is true of the equatorial type of sundial).

All sundials have one point in common: the indicating arm or 'style' must lie parallel to the Earth's axis, and point in the direction of the celestial pole, marked approximately, in northern latitudes, by Polaris. The indicator is aligned at an angle corresponding to the latitude of the site, and is pointed due north.

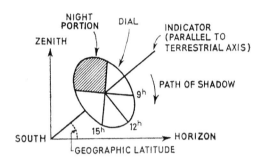

Fig. 16. A simple equatorial sundial.

The equatorial sundial—probably the simplest kind—is shown in Fig. 16. The dial is a circular disc, divided into 24 sectors (15 degrees apart). The indicator is fixed at the centre, and the whole instrument tilted at the appropriate angle, determined by the latitude. The plane of the dial then lies parallel to that of the equator. An important point to remember is that the opposite applies south of the equator, and in the tropics both sides of the dial have to be calibrated, to allow for the fact that the Sun changes from one side of the celestial equator to the other.

The accuracy to which a sundial may be read depends, to some considerable extent, upon its size. The greater the diameter of the dial, the more important it becomes to ensure that the style is located precisely at the centre. If the dial is to be marked off in quarter-hour intervals, or even in minutes, the diameter should be at least 18 inches. The well-known expert Lothar M. Loske, of Mexico City, gives the following example*: 'The first action when marking off the dial is to calculate the circumference. Suppose that the diameter is 50 cm. (approximately 18 inches); the length of the circumference is then $50 \times 3 \cdot 1416 = 159 \cdot 08$ cm (since circumference $= 2\pi r$). Dividing this by 2 gives us the path of the shadow from 6 a.m. to 6 p.m. ($= 79 \cdot 54$ cm). If we now divide this by 12, we obtain the distance through which the shadow has to travel at the perimeter from hour to hour. This works out at $66 \cdot 3$ cm. It is then easy enough to work out that the calibrations to indicate minutes have to be $1 \cdot 1$ mm apart. Because of the fine divisions, a delicate style is necessary, as otherwise the shadow cast will be inconveniently broad; a thin wire is very suitable.'

Horizontal sundials are suitable for gardens and parks, but if the sundial is to be fixed to the side of a building it should be of the vertical type. If the selected wall faces due south, the whole matter becomes relatively simple.

Let us look first at Fig. 17, and then examine the instructions in detail. From a centre A a semicircle is drawn, the radius depending on the amount of space available. Next draw a horizontal line at a tangent to this semicircle, and touching it at B. AB will be vertical,

---

* For further details about sundials and their construction, see L. M. Loske, *Die Sonnenuhren* (Springer-Verlag, 1959). This is in German. Readers who do not read German will find details in the book by R. N. and M. L. Mayall, *Sundials, How to know, Use and Make them.*

and thus perpendicular to the horizontal tangent. Now we divide the semicircle into 12 equal sectors: $180°/12 = 15°$. The radii from A are produced to meet the east–west axis.

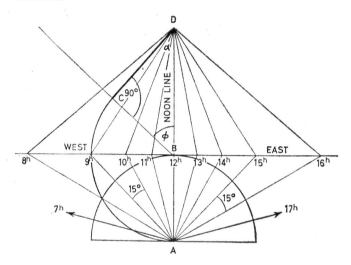

Fig. 17. Drawing up the dial of a vertical sundial. ϕ = geographic latitude.

From B we construct an angle equivalent to the latitude of the site. If not already known, this can be found from a large-scale map, or by consulting the local Public Library, where the information will certainly be found.

With AB as radius we next draw an arc from centre B, giving us point C. Constructing the perpendicular at C and extending it in an upward direction so that it intersects AB produced at D, we find the point at which the indicator must be fixed. CD in fact represents the indicator, which must now be pointed south, making sure that it remains at 90 degrees *minus* the geographic latitude (angle a).

Building a Sundial

The next task is to join D to the hour intervals marked on the east-west axis, and to number them. AD is the noon line, and to the west of this will lie the morning hours, the afternoon hours lying to the east. There is no real need to mark all the hours, and it is enough to mark those for that part of the day when the sundial will be useful.

Complications are introduced if the building to which the sundial is to be fixed does not face precisely south. In this brief account we cannot deal with these difficulties —and much more remains to be said; for instance, I have not attempted to deal with details of the equation of time. However, all the relevant information will be found in the books by Loske or Mayall, and all I have tried to do here is to give a very short introduction to the subject.

Anyone who builds a sundial will produce a piece of apparatus which is not only of astronomical use, but is also ornamental and aesthetically pleasing. The materials available are many; metal (bronze, brass, aluminium, stainless steel, etc.) for the dial and indicator, or—for the dial—stone, mosaic, hardwood or even a mixture of several materials. The choice is wide open, with the reservation that the sundial must be able to withstand all the vagaries of the climate.

Sol omnibus lucet—the Sun shines for all, but, perhaps, particularly for the amateur astronomer. The Sun gives us light and warmth; it also tells us the time, and the sundial is a symbol of the Sun's never-ending journey along the ecliptic.

Conclusion

The aim of this book has been to offer the reader a few samples from the wide field of the science of astronomy, in which the amateur can actively participate. Full participation entails not merely study from the academic point of view, but also active and actual observation. I therefore hope that the samples offered will have whetted the reader's appetite sufficiently to make him want to set about doing something for himself.

In these few pages it has obviously not been possible to cover all aspects. There is more, a great deal more, for the amateur to discover with the aid of his telescope. The subjects which I have chosen are not necessarily better than others which I have failed to mention, but to my mind they will give the would-be observer a good general grounding in practical astronomy. The sort of work which any one amateur astronomer will want to undertake depends largely on the opportunity he has for carrying on his observations and where his particular interests lie.

There is a wealth of literature on astronomy in general, as well as on specific aspects. The bibliography which follows indicates some of the works which may be found helpful; a complete list is not only out of the question, but simply to read everything that has ever been written about the subject would allow the reader no time for his own practical observations. Personal experience teaches us something which cannot be learned in any other way, and the encouragement *to see for oneself* is worth while passing on from one generation to the next.

Appendix I

(a) MAGNIFICATION (see page 14)

Objective		Eyepiece					
Aperture	Focal length						
mm	mm	Focal length	40 mm	25 mm	15 mm	10 mm	5 mm
50	500	Magnifica-tions	12×	20×	33×	50×	100×
50	750		19×	30×	50×	75×	150×
100	1000		25×	40×	66×	100×	200×
100	1500		37×	60×	100×	150×	300×
150	2250		56×	90×	150×	225×	450×

(b) EYEPIECES AND THE FIELD OF VISION (see page 38)

Type of eyepiece	Magnifications						
	20×	50×	75×	100×	150×	200×	
Huyghenian	140′	60′	40′	30′	20′	15′	Field of vision in minutes of arc
Orthoscopic	120′	50′	30′	25′	15′	11′	
Monocentric	90′	35′	24′	17′	11′	9′	

Appendix II

Using Setting Circles and Calculating Sidereal Time (see p. 28)

Using Setting Circles and Calculating
Sidereal Time (see p. 28)

To obtain the correct setting two factors have to be considered:

1. the Sidereal Hour Angle (SHA) t
2. the angle of declination δ

For a given body we can look up the following co-ordinates in a handbook, or almanac:

1. right ascension α
2. declination δ

The declination circle can now be set to the relevant value without further calculation, but right ascension must first be converted into the hour angle, t. This we can accomplish by means of Sidereal Time Ⓗ using the equation:

Hour Angle = Sidereal Time − Right Ascension

or $\mathbf{t} = Ⓗ − \alpha$

For anyone fortunate enough to possess a clock which registers Sidereal Time this conversion is a simple matter, but failing this one must needs calculate Sidereal Time for oneself; here again, two factors have to be considered:

1. Sidereal Time for midnight at Greenwich, which will be found in the handbook;
2. Any difference between Standard, or Zone Time and the real, or local time of the observing station.

The Sidereal Day is 3 min 55·91 sec shorter than our normal, solar day. Also there is a difference between Sidereal and normal time corresponding to the difference in longitude between the observing station and Greenwich, which must be taken into account:

    1. *east* of Greenwich such difference must be *subtracted*;
    2. *west* of Greenwich such difference must be *added*.

Thus:
Sidereal Time for midnight at Greenwich ± the difference in respect of longitude gives us Sidereal Time for midnight at observing station.

Midnight for observing station = o hr o min o sec local time ± any difference between Standard, or Zone Time and local time (zonal time might, for instance, be Central European Time, i.e. one hour in advance of GMT and equivalent to British Summer Time). We now have the values for:

    1. Sidereal Time for midnight at observing station;
    2. Zonal Time for midnight at observing station.

Let us now suppose that the following values apply for these:

Midnight at observing station
              = o hr o min o sec local time
              = o hr 10 min 10 sec CET
              = 4 hr 30 min 20 sec Sidereal Time

However, the observation is to be made not at midnight, but at 4 a.m. Central European Time. The interval between o hr 10 min 10 sec CET and 4 hr o min o sec CET is 3 hr 49 min 50 sec of normal time, but, because Sidereal Time gains 9.9 sec during each normal hour, the value

expressed in terms of Sidereal Time is 3 hr 50 min 29 sec
(= 3 hr 49 min 50 sec + approx. 4 × 9·9 sec).

If we now add:

      4 hr 30 min 20 sec Sidereal Time (see above)

+ 3 hr 50 min 29 sec Sidereal Time

    8 hr 20 min 49 sec Sidereal Time

and this value is the Sidereal Time for our example observation time, 4 a.m. Central European Time. It now
remains for us to substitute this value for Ⓗ in the equation for finding the hour angle, viz.

$$t = 8 \text{ hr } 20 \text{ min } 49 \text{ sec } - a$$

Appendix III

FORMULÆ FOR ASTROPHOTOGRAPHY (see pp. 103 and 124)

1. In astronomical photography one must always take into account the fact that the diurnal rotation of the Earth upon its axis causes all celestial bodies to appear to move across the sky from east to west. In one second of time a given star will thus appear to move through the angle:

$$\frac{360°}{23 \text{ hr } 56 \text{ min } 4 \cdot 091 \text{ sec}} = 0 \cdot 004°$$

An objective having a focal length of 100 mm will portray an angle of 1° as an image 1·8 mm long. At such focal length, therefore, a given star will trace an image 0·0072 mm long on the negative in one second. If the camera is static, the resolving power of the emulsion lies at 0·03 mm.

2. For photographs taken at the focus of an objective having a diameter D and a focal length f the exposure time is t:

$$t = t_0 \left(\frac{D_0 f}{f_0 D} \right)^2$$

Here t_0 is the known exposure time for the same body with an objective D_0/f_0.

3. The diameter of an image at the focus of a telescope $= f . \tan \alpha$; where f is the focal length of the objective and α the angular diameter of the object to be portrayed.

Appendix III

4. The following table gives the magnitudes of the faintest objects it is possible to register on 18 DIN emulsions under average atmospheric conditions, together with the maximum exposure times (minutes) required:

Aperture in mm	$f = 1:2$ Max. exposure	Faintest objects	$f = 1:5$ Max. exposure	Faintest objects
50	35 min	13^m	300 min	15^m
100	35 min	14^m	300 min	16^m
150	35 min	$14·5^m$	300 min	$16·5^m$
200	35 min	15^m	300 min	17^m

Appendix IV

With the aid of a spectroscopic eyepiece, consisting of a five-element Amici Prism for direct viewing, it is possible to examine the spectra of bright stars. Tabulated below are some facts and figures for several prominent celestial objects:

Star	R.A. (for 1950)	Dec.	Magnitude	Spectral class	Remarks
ε Orionis	5 h 33·7 m	×01° 13′	1·7^m	B O	Absorption lines of helium and hydrogen
α Canis Maj. (Sirius)	6 h 42·9 m	−16° 39′	−1·4^m	A O	Distinct absorption lines of hydrogen
α Canis Min. (Procyon)	7 h 36·7 m	+05° 21′	0·4^m	F 5	Calcium lines; hydrogen lines recede
α Aurigæ (Capella)	5 h 13 m	+45° 57′	0·1^m	G 1	Very distinct calcium lines
α Bootis (Arcturus)	14 h 13·4 m	+19° 27′	0·0^m	K 2	Ammonium, hydrocarbons and water vapour
α Orionis (Betelgeux)	5 h 52·5 m	+07° 24′	0·1–1·2^m	M 2	Titanium oxide bands more strongly developed

The absorption lines which are characteristic of the

above spectra are distributed through each spectrum as follows:

Element	Region of spectrum
Calcium lines	Extreme violet
Hydrogen lines H δ	Violet
Ammonium, hycrocarbons and water vapour	Blue
Hydrogen line H γ	Blue
Hydrogen line H β	Blue-green
Titanium oxide bands	Green

Appendix V

I. SOME USEFUL DOUBLE STARS FOR TEST PURPOSES (see p. 51)

Star	R.A. 1960	Dec.	Magnitude	Separation distance 1960	Position 1960	Remarks
ε Hyades	8 h 45 m	+06·6°	3·5ᵐ/6·9ᵐ	3·06″	269° 3·0″	Not difficult for 2-inch instrument
ι Cassiopeiae	2 h 26 m	+67·2°	4·7ᵐ/7·6ᵐ	2·30″	238° 2·3″	Just possible for 2-inch
μ Draconis	17 h 04 m	+54·5°	5·8ᵐ/5·8ᵐ	2·04″	74° 2·1″	Simple for 3-inch
μ Cygni	21 h 42 m	+28·6°	4·7ᵐ/6·1ᵐ	1·42″	282° 1·6″	Just possible for 3-inch. Already creditable performance for 4-inch
λ Cygni	20 h 46 m	+36·3°	4·7ᵐ/6·0ᵐ	0·81″	25° 0·8″	Just possible for 6-inch

2. Some Variables for Estimating Steps (see p. 113)

Star	R.A. 1950	Dec.	Magnitude max.	Magnitude min.	Period in days	Discovery Year	Discovery Discoverer
o Ceti (Mira)	2 h 16·8 m	−3° 12′	2·0^m	10·1^m	331·6	1596	Fabricius
β Persei (Algol)	3 h 4·9 m	+40° 46′	2·2^m	3·5^m	2·8673	1667	Montanari
λ Tauri	5 h 57·9 m	+12° 21′	3·8^m	4·1^m	3·95295	1848	Baxendell
ζ Geminorum	7 h 1·2 m	+20° 39′	3·7^m	4·3^m	10·1510	1847	Schmidt
β Lyrae	18 h 48·2 m	+33° 18′	3·4^m	4·3^m	12·9301	1784	Goodrike
η Aquilae	19 h 49·9 m	+01° 01′	3·7^m	4·4^m	7·1767	1784	Pigott
δ Cephei	22 h 27·3 m	+58° 09′	3·7^m	4·9^m	5·3663	1784	Goodrike

Some Standard Stellar Magnitudes (see p. 115)

It is a good exercise to find, and remember the magnitude of, each of the stars listed below. So far as possible they have been chosen for ease of location, and also because the difference in brightness between one star and the next is roughly 0·5^m. The exact positions will be found on any star map.

Star	Proper name	Magnitude
α Geminorum	Castor	1·58
α Ursæ Majoris	Dubhe	2·00
γ Ursæ Majoris	Phad	2·54
β Draconis	Alwaid	2·99
δ Ursæ Majoris	Megrez	3·44
β Aquilæ	Alshain (near Altair)	3·90
δ Ursæ Minoris	Yildun (near Polaris)	4·44
η Ursæ Minoris	Alasco	5·04

Appendix VI

A α	Alpha		*N* ν	Nu	
B β	Beta		*Ξ* ξ	Xi or Si	
Γ γ	Gamma		*O* o	Omicron	
Δ δ	Delta		*Π* π	Pi	
E ε	Epsilon		*P* ϱ	Rho	
Z ζ	Zeta		*Σ* σ ς	Sigma	
H η	Eta		*T* τ	Tau	
Θ θ	Theta		*Y* υ	Upsilon	
I ι	Iota		*Φ* φ	Phi	
K ϰ	Kappa		*X* χ	Chi	
Λ λ	Lambda		*Ψ* ψ	Psi	
M μ	Mu		*Ω* ω	Omega	

List of Books and Societies

I. GENERAL BOOKS

J. B. Sidgwick: *Amateur Astronomers' Handbook*, Faber & Faber, 1958 (3rd edition).
A comprehensive account of the optical and technical knowledge required by active amateur astronomers. The book contains many illustrations and diagrams, and has a good bibliography.

J. B. Sidgwick: *Observational Astronomy for Amateurs*, Faber & Faber, 1957 (2nd edition).
An introduction and guide to the observation of various celestial subjects, and there is also a list of relevant publications.

P. Moore: *The Amateur Astronomer*, Lutterworth Press, 1961 (4th edition).
An ideal book for the beginner as well as the more practised amateur observer. The book contains a number of useful appendices and a bibliography which lists the works under various subject headings.

II. HANDBOOKS

Handbook of the British Astronomical Association, edited by C. Dinwoodie, is a useful publication for amateurs.

Yearbook of Astronomy, edited by J. G. Porter, is published annually by Eyre & Spottiswoode. This is a book which will appeal to all amateur observers, especially those interested in the planets. It gives a month-by-month account of what is to be seen, where and at what times. It also contains a number of up-to-date articles on various aspects of astronomy, as well as a list of astronomical societies, both national and local.

The Astronomical Ephemeris, published annually in London and Washington since 1959. It replaces two former publications, *The Nautical Almanac* (U.K.) and the *American Ephemeris* (U.S.A.). This handbook contains information about everything likely to happen in the Solar System during the year. However, this book will probably appeal more to the really advanced observer.

Brown's Almanac contains many useful tables and copies of this book will be found in the reference section of most Public Libraries.

There are also several other handbooks issued not only by national organisations, but also by local societies and observatories in Britain, Canada and the U.S.A.

III. PERIODICALS

Sky and Telescope, edited by Ch. A. Federer, Jr., Harvard College Observatory, published by the Sky Publishing Corporation, Cambridge, Mass. This comes out monthly and deals with all aspects of astronomy.

Journal of the British Astronomical Association, issued by the B.A.A. each month, also deals with all branches of astronomy.

Astronomical periodicals of a general nature are also published in France, Germany, Holland, Belgium, Denmark and Sweden, and those interested can probably find out more about them at their local Public Libraries.

List of Books and Societies

British Astronomical Association, founded in 1890, is the leading society for amateur observers in the English-speaking world. The secretarial address is: Burlington House, Piccadilly, London, W.1.

Junior Astronomical Society exists principally for young observers of school age, and publishes its own quarterly journal. The society also has a number of local branches. The secretarial address is: 44 Cedar Way, Basingstoke, Hants.

Amateur Astronomers' Association of New York. This society operates in conjunction with the New York Planetarium. The offices are at: 223 West 79th Street, New York 24, N.Y., U.S.A.

Association of Lunar and Planetary Observers is a leading international society for amateur observers. Secretarial address: Pan American College Observatory, Edinburg, Texas, U.S.A.

Vereinigung der Sternfreunde e. V., founded in 1952, is the society for German amateurs. Address: München 9, Theodolindenstrasse 6, W. Germany*.

There are also many local astronomical societies and a fairly comprehensive list of these can be found in *The Yearbook of Astronomy* mentioned above.

N.B. When entering into correspondence with any of these societies *please* enclose a stamped addressed envelope, or, if writing abroad, an International Reply Coupon.

* All general queries and particularly requests dealing with German astronomical publications and German astronomical instruments and optics, will be answered by the General Secretary at this address.

Index

151

Index